Hangman

The Life and Crimes of
Gerard John Schaefer Jr.

by

Michael Newton

Hangman

The Life and Crimes of Gerard John Schaefer Jr.

by

Michael Newton

ISBN-13: 978-1987902167
ISBN-10: 1987902165

Copyright and Published (10.2016)
by RJ Parker Publishing, Inc.

Published in United States of America

Copyrights

This book is licensed for your personal enjoyment only. All rights reserved. No part of this publication can be reproduced or transmitted in any form or by any means without prior written authorization from RJ Parker Publishing, Inc. The unauthorized reproduction or distribution of a copyrighted work is illegal. Criminal copyright infringement, including infringement without monetary gain, is investigated by the FBI and is punishable by fines and federal imprisonment.

"This is a work of nonfiction. No names have been changed, no characters invented, no events fabricated."

– RJ Parker, PhD

More True Crime Books in the Kindle Store:

__rjpp.ca/RJ-PARKER-BOOKS__

Table of Contents

Dedicated to Dave Frasier. One for the road, old friend.

Preface: The Psycho Who Sued Me

In June 1993 I received notice by certified mail that Florida prison inmate No. 035906 was suing me in federal court, alleging that brief mention of him in a book I'd published three years earlier had libeled him and harmed his prospects for parole from his life sentence on two counts of kidnapping and murdering young women. At the time, he had served 20 years, with no parole hearings in sight.

The notice came as no particular surprise. I'd corresponded with Gerard Schaefer Jr. for several months, at first through his ex-girlfriend-turned-publisher, then directly to and from the state prison that housed him at Raiford, in Union County. During our exchange of letters, he had denied any killings and pitched the tale of himself as an honorable lawman framed by crooked colleagues for uncovering their ties to drug cartels. Whoever killed the women he stood trial for, they had been "drug snitches." When I preferred to tell his story as revealed in legal documents, Schaefer sent warnings of costly legal action ahead should I defy him and neglect to tell what he called his "True Story."

In fact, among his other claims to infamy, Schaefer was well known for serial litigation, harassing journalists who summoned the temerity to mention him in print. He sued another author in the same week that he filed on me. A second case of *Schaefer v. Newton* followed in 1994, when he learned that I had named him in one sentence from another book, published in 1992. Again, he claimed his "civil rights" were violated, his parole delayed—a claim I easily disproved by contacting each member of the Florida Commission of Inmate Review, receiving their assurances that they had never read my books nor even heard of me at all. If that were not enough, his first theoretical parole date was in February 2017, a quarter century after he sued me for "delaying" it.

Still it was necessary to proceed with foiling Schaefer at his game. Federal courts take inmate allegations of abuse quite seriously, as they should, and so the case dragged on for 13 months before Judge William Elwood Steckler. Along the way, Schaefer withdrew his second case, for reasons I would only later learn, then lost the first with a decisive ruling in my favor. Another case, against a British author, saw him labeled "libel proof." But still, it seemed that he would always find a new excuse to sue again, billing taxpayers for his folly.

And then, a few months later, he was dead, hacked to death in his cell by a fellow inmate and multiple murderer, serving life plus 20 years for two slayings committed in 1990. The story should have ended there. And yet, the saga of his sickness still goes on.

Hangman follows the course of Schaefer's twisted life and crimes from cradle to grave, exploring his family background, education, psychological evaluations, and evidence of escalating violence from his failed ambitions to become a priest, then a teacher, finally a law enforcement officer. While he attained the last position, Schaefer's brooding aberrations ultimately drove him to destroy himself. And even then, confined for life, his predatory urges found their outlet through continuing harassment via mail, litigation, and jailhouse informing.

The story that follows is true. No conversations have been "reconstructed" in *Hangman,* no secret thoughts divined by posthumous armchair psychoanalysis. Any dialogue presented has been quoted from persons involved, to the best of their recollection. Schaefer's private correspondence, placed in the public domain as evidence in *Schaefer v. Newton,* speaks for itself. There is no need to dramatize the hangman's crimes.

The truth is bad enough.

Chapter 1: Making A Murderer

Gerard John Schaefer Jr. was born on March 25, 1946, in Neenah, Wisconsin, some 40 miles southwest of Green Bay, in Winnebago County. It stands near the southern end of Little Lake Butte des Morts—"Mound of the Dead" as translated from French—which seems in retrospect to be prophetic. Neenah's best-known resident, prior to Schaefer, was Charles Benjamin Clark, co-founder of Kimberly-Clark Corporation and later a 19th-century U.S. congressman.

Coincidentally, Gerard Sr. worked as a traveling salesman for Kimberly-Clark, peddling their products that included Kotex feminine napkins (developed in 1920) and Kleenex tissues (since 1926). With wife Doris, he called their first child "John" around the house, and two more followed in due time: daughter Sara, four years younger than Gerard, and son Gary, five years after Sara. While Doris later described her first-born's childhood as "idyllic" and deemed him "just like any other kid," Gerard Jr. felt otherwise. In the 1970s, he described himself to court-appointed psychiatrists as an "illegitimate" child, the unwanted product of a "forced wedding." He claimed his parents never had a good relationship, adding that his father "was always critical" of him, while Doris was "always on my back to do better." Childhood, in Junior's view, was "turbulent and conflictual." As his sixth birthday approached, Gerard Sr. was frequently absent, beginning the long slide into alcoholism and flagrant adultery.

Worse yet was young Gerard's belief that his father favored sister Sara, viewing his elder son with disdain. That perceived slight seemed to divide Junior's psyche. At times, he wished to be a girl; at others, he contemplated suicide. "I wanted to die," he told analysts. "I couldn't please my father, so in playing games I always got killed." By adolescence, he would graduate to sadomasochism, including self-bondage. From sixth grade (age 12) onward, Schaefer said, "I'd tie myself to a tree, struggle to get free, and I'd get excited sexually and do something to hurt myself." More specifically, the "hurt" included masturbation coupled with fantasies of "hurting other people, women in particular." At the same age, he went on, "I discovered women's underwear—panties. Sometimes I wore them." And again, "I'd want to hurt myself."

Schaefer's parents raised him as a Catholic, immersed in faith despite a failure to reflect those principles at home. He survived a bout of scarlet fever at age four, not always true in 1950, and entered elementary school at the usual age, hiding his precocious fascination with death that reached a point where he sometimes couldn't distinguish fact from fantasy. After he

11

graduated from sixth grade, Kimberly-Clark transferred his father to Atlanta, Georgia, where they spent the next two years.

In autumn 1958, Schaefer enrolled at the Marist School on Ivy Street (now Peachtree Center Avenue), a Roman Catholic preparatory institution founded in 1901 by the Society of Mary. Famed alumni of the school include golf legend Bobby Jones, actor/singer David Hasselhoff, television's longtime "Miss America" host Bert Parks—and excised from the institution's list of treasured students, one David Reed Fields, future founder of the neo-Nazi National States Rights Party. Schaefer met none of them but did his best at academics while expanding his autoerotic sexual repertoire.

Atlanta was merely a pit stop for Gerard Sr.'s odyssey with Kimberly-Clark. In 1960, the family moved once again, this time to Fort Lauderdale, Florida, where Schaefer's parents promptly joined yachting and country clubs. Gerard Jr. enrolled as a freshman at Saint Thomas Aquinas High School, opened in 1936 with only 12 students, run under the aegis of the Dominican Sisters from Adrian, Michigan. The school's motto: "Not for school but for life we learn." Yearbooks from Schaefer's tenure at St. Thomas Aquinas list him as a member of the football team during his second and third years, but no one recalls him taking the field or joining in any other group activity. Ex-classmates remember him as a loner, branded "weird" and "out of it." One claimed he would "practically stand on his head to see up a girl's skirt." In class, he angered nuns by challenging religious dogma and once penned an essay scientifically refuting the virgin birth of Jesus.

Schaefer made a few friends, though. The only two identified in print to date were Mike McGonigle and John "Jack" Dolan. Oddly, in their high school days, neither considered Schaefer a close friend, though Dolan sometimes double-dated with the future Hangman. Schaefer kept in touch with both, sporadically, serving as best man at McGonigle's wedding in 1968. Dolan joined the Navy after high school, touring the world, but he met Schaefer again at college and would briefly share a house with him in 1970 under disturbing circumstances.

After hours, Schaefer hewed to the school's motto, learning for life.

His most influential instructor was Schaefer's first sexual partner, generally called "Cindy" in his letters, or "C. W.," and sometimes "Cass." In later psychiatric interviews, the Hangman called Cindy "extremely intelligent," but she wears a different face in his private correspondence, placed in the public domain as federal court exhibits. Despite attending daily mass throughout high school, he led another life at night. As he wrote in November 1991: "C. W. was a sexual disaster area who literally couldn't come unless she was slapped into insensibility, her clothing actually ripped off her back and her ass; all the while hearing what a dirty little wet assed slut she was, a rotten little sex slut on her way to Hell, etc. etc. After a few years of that I knew my way around masochistic females. That's not my erotic tastes [*sic*] personally but I was interested in it academically."

And in another letter on Cindy: "She was a pure maso and trained my teen self to be her sado partner. Classic pattern. Masos (called 'Bottoms' in the freak life) call the scenarios and require a partner who has good *control* to interact with. (Sados are called 'Toppers.') By the time I was 17 I was a skilled 'topper'—thanks to C. W. There was real conflict because I'm not a true Topper...I'm a natural romantic so Sado went against my emotional grain however I *did* freak with C. W. regularly."

At least, that is, until his senior year, when —as a psychiatrist reported in 1973—Cindy "went off to college and left him. That day he went into the woods and tied himself with a rope to the trees and hurt himself in the masochistic way he used to do when he was younger. This was the first time in more than two years."

Which, if we believe Schaefer's report, meant that he continued playing "maso" for over a year after beginning his four years of "sado" rape fantasies with Cindy. Who was teaching whom?

14

Twenty-seven years after their breakup, Schaefer wrote that serial killing "was simply carrying the topper role beyond the parameters of the scene. Easy to do emotionally if you are a veteran topper."

And one driven by bloodlust, at that.

Decades later, controversy would surround the date of Schaefer's first murder. In various letters and pieces of "killer fiction," he first claimed 1965, then pushed his start-up date back to 1962, at age 16. In one published tale, Schaefer said his first murder was "accidental," that he'd found himself surprised to have strangled a girl while "fooling around" with a garrote. Later in the same piece, he claimed seven kills before he first had "normal sex" with a girl, but stopped short of saying whether he meant with Cindy or the high school student who later replaced her. After Schaefer's death, Detective Dave Kelly from North Miami Beach reportedly told author Sondra London, "I personally believe Schaefer was responsible for a lot more crimes than he was confined for...I believe he probably started his activities in his early teen years, probably 12 to 14, and I'm talking murder, not just his sexual activities."

True or not, Schaefer concealed his virulent rage for the most part—that is, until he met a girl from whom he could not altogether hide.

*****

In spring 1964, Schaefer attended a high school dance where he met brunette Sandy Stewart, one year his junior at age 17. Stewart admits being swept off her feet by the "dazzling young stranger," as she described Schaefer. At the evening's end, she declined to give him her phone number but told him her surname. The next day, Schaefer plowed through Fort Lauderdale's phone book, dialing each Stewart in turn until he found the right number and asked Sandy out on a date. Three decades later, she wrote, "I was flattered by his attention at the time, but looking back I realize that was an indication of how thorough and persistent he could be when tracking down a female that excited him."

And Schaefer *was* excited. He became Stewart's first lover, impressing her as sensitive and enthusiastic, eager to please. There was no hint of "top" or "bottom" in their pairing, though it did have humorous moments—like the night a shore patrol with spotlights caught Schaefer and Stewart naked on the beach. Instead of cringing, Stewart recalled leaping to her feet, with no attempt to hide herself, telling the officers, "We were finished, anyway!"

Schaefer concealed that passion when he met Sandy's parents, an insurance salesman and a homemaker who served as president of the local Parent-Teacher Association. When visiting their home, Schaefer wowed her parents with his impeccable manners, often joining them for dinner and reportedly accompanying the Stewarts on at least one holiday vacation. Other times, he took Sandy into the Everglades, where Schaefer loved to spend time hunting and fishing. When she couldn't bring herself to kill an animal for "sport," he seemed amused, but didn't press the issue.

Life seemed perfect through early summer 1964, after John graduated from Saint Thomas Aquinas and began considering his higher education options. Sandy had another year ahead of her at Stranahan High School, but Fort Lauderdale and its surrounding cities teemed with colleges, if Schaefer planned on staying close to home. Close to his steady girl.

Yet cracks had opened, both in Schaefer's mind and in the apple pie façade he had erected to encircle his relationship with Sandy Stewart. Schaefer felt tectonic plates of madness slipping, letting rancid fumes escape. Before long, Sandy caught the scent as well.

Chapter 2: College Boy

If any doubts remained concerning Schaefer's psychosexual confusion after high school, he put them to rest at age 18. Despite his ongoing affair with Sandy Stewart, he decided against moving on to college after graduation, opting to become a priest instead. His chosen training ground was Saint John Vianney College Seminary, a Catholic institution founded in 1959 by Miami's first Archbishop, Coleman Carroll. The seminary says its mission is "to form men for the diocesan priesthood by focusing on the pillars of formation: human, spiritual, pastoral, and academic." Planted on Miami's outskirts when the Magic City's first archdiocese was formed, Saint John Vianney opened its chapel in 1964, just as Schaefer prepared to adopt a celibate life.

But it was not to be.

The seminary turned him down, and while their reasons were not publicly disclosed, Schaefer himself would summarize them nine years later, speaking to a court-appointed psychiatrist. "They said I didn't have enough faith," he recalled, admitting that rejection from the priesthood made him quit the Church of Rome. "I didn't think it was fair," he declared.

On balance, it was just as well. The church faced ample scandals in the years ahead, without having the Hangman on its payroll.

*****

September 1964 found Schaefer enrolled at Broward Community College, opened in 1960 as the Junior College of Broward County, with a faculty of 28 serving 701 students. Builders completed the school's first permanent buildings three years later, shifting students from the former Naval Air Station Junior High buildings on the western fringe of Fort Lauderdale-Hollywood International Airport. Schaefer turned in a mediocre academic performance in his first semester at BCC, though he enjoyed English classes taught by novelist Harry Crews, often cited by Schaefer in later years as an inspiration for his own unique style of writing.

English aside, Schaefer preferred hunting in the Everglades to study. He continued dating Sandy Stewart, but for her, their relationship felt more like therapy than romance, with Schaefer pouring out his angry, often tearful revelations of an urge to kill the "evil" women who aroused him. One such was Leigh Hainline, a neighbor and sometime tennis partner two years his senior, who allegedly stripped before her open bedroom window to taunt him. Another female neighbor of Schaefer's had the temerity to sunbathe in her own front yard, thus "flaunting" herself to infuriate him.

For the sunbather—never identified—he had worked out a detailed plan, telling Sandy that he planned to club her with a baseball bat, wrap her in a blanket, and convey her to the Everglades in his father's boat, where he would shoot her and leave her for the alligators. According to Stewart, Schaefer never killed that neighbor but "actually did sexually assault her," later recording the details in a work of "fiction" titled "Gator Bait." That story describes the first-person narrator inflamed by a neighbor's near-nudity in a bikini, invading her home by night and catching her asleep, holding her at knifepoint while he masturbates onto her buttocks, then urinates around her head on a pillow, before choking her unconscious, writing "whore" on her back with lipstick, and stealing money from her purse. In "Gator Bait," Schaefer described his "overwhelming sense of guilt," noting that he "was still young then, and unacquainted with the parameters of power and rage in the unholy union between sexual release and death." After the attack, the neighbor still sunbathed, but safely concealed in her backyard.

There was rage enough in Schaefer's mind to go around, from telling Sandy of the rape games he had played with girlfriend Cindy, to the screaming confrontations with his father, sometimes ending in physical violence. At last, in summer 1965, Sandy was fed up enough to dump him. Schaefer pined and stalked her, watching her on dates with other boys, sending her notes with third-rate doggerel—then, as he later told Dr. Mordecai Haber, "I started to take it out on myself. I became a masochist." Specifically, he'd once again tie himself to trees, a rope around his waist, and masturbate while struggling to free himself. Soon, he graduated to attacks on livestock, telling Dr. Haber, "I'd cut them up, cut off their heads with a machete, and have intercourse with them."

Back at BCC in autumn 1965, Schaefer remained distracted but signed up for creative writing, taught by Betty Owens, who deemed him "a very promising writer," welcoming his submissions of prose and poetry to *P'an-Ku,* BCC's literary and arts magazine. Schaefer briefly dated a girl named Judy Hancock and reportedly moonlighted as Emergency Room security at the Broward County Medical Center. Still, homicidal fantasies deluged him, and he finally confessed them to Betty Owens. The victim he had in mind, Schaefer said, was a younger female BCC teacher. Owens referred Schaefer to Dr. Neil Crispo, Director of Student Activities, for help. As Crispo recalled their meeting to the *Miami Herald,* Schaefer omitted mention of his wish to kill a teacher, digressing to discuss joining the U.S. Army.

"I asked him why he wanted to join," Crispo recalled. "He said he 'would like to kill things.' He said, 'I even like to shoot at cows now.' He said he hadn't killed any cows, though."

At least, not with a gun.

Crispo referred Schaefer to Dr. Adolph Koch, a BCC psychology professor, who later had no memory of meeting Schaefer, although he told Crispo that "someone from the school psychology department had contacted Schaefer's mother." Doris Schaefer thought it was Koch himself who recommended treatment for her son at the Henderson Mental Health Center in Lauderdale Lakes, whose services include walk-in evaluation and treatment, crisis counseling, short-term psychotherapy, and a first episode psychosis program that seeks "to alter the course and prognosis of schizophrenia by providing rapid, comprehensive, effective treatment at the early stages of psychosis."

After Gerard presented himself at the clinic, Doris told the *Herald,* "I asked the psychiatrist what John's problem was, but he said he couldn't tell me. He said, 'If I disclose anything to you, you'll be looking for something. You might be overly suspicious.' He said I should leave him alone and not bug him." Meanwhile, she said, "The psychiatrist told him to write down everything that went through his mind. It was supposed to help him somehow."

Instead, Schaefer's writings would help convict him of murder.

Decades later, Schaefer would blame Sandy Stewart for his descent into sadism and homicide. "I will tell you here and now," he wrote, "that plenty of young women died because you couldn't help me solve my various crises in 1965. I tried to tell you about it but you couldn't deal with it. You bolted, abandoned me; that's when it started."

*****

Schaefer completed one semester at BCC in 1965 before he found a new preoccupation, in the form of "Moral Rearmament." Founded in May 1938, the movement was initially a response to depression-era militarization in Europe. Leader Frank Buchman declared, "The crisis is fundamentally a moral one. The nations must re-arm morally. Moral recovery is essentially the forerunner of economic recovery. Moral recovery creates not crisis but confidence and unity in every phase of life." Instead, World War II erupted, but Buchman's movement survived, circling the globe by the 1960s, when Buchman proclaimed, "MRA is the good road of an ideology inspired by God upon which all can unite. Catholic, Jew and Protestant, Hindu, Muslim, Buddhist and Confucianist, all find they can change, where needed, and travel along this good road together."

Part of that "good road" in the 1960s was Up With People, a traveling musical troupe that aimed to bridge cultural barriers and create global understanding. In early 1966, the clean-cut, super-patriotic troubadours hit BCC, billing themselves as "Sing Out '66." Along with rousing anthems such as "Freedom Isn't Free," they urged student listeners to quit school and join them on tour. Schaefer took the bait and traveled with the group from February through July because, in the words of friend Mike McGonigle, "He thought they looked like kids who were doing something good for America."

One of Schaefer's fellow cast members was 19-year-old Glenn Close, a future Broadway and Hollywood actress with three Emmys, three Tonys and six Academy Award nominations to her credit. Close viewed Moral Rearmament and its spin-offs as "a cult group" that consumed her family for 15 years before their final breakaway, fighting "to survive the pressures of a culture that dictated everything about how we lived our lives." Another of the singers, closer to Schaefer, was Massachusetts native Martha "Marty" Fogg (misnamed as "Marion" in some accounts). They seemed to mesh, but Martha was the product of a strict upbringing and left him sexually frustrated. He may have hoped for more on Sing Out's European summer tour, but as mother Doris related, "He got the measles."

*****

Back at BCC again in autumn 1966, Schaefer completed that school year without another interruption and sat through an eight-week 1967 summer term to graduate with an associate degree in business administration that he'd never use. Unknown to those around him, he had crossed the line from killing livestock to pursuit of humans—and not always single victims. Long afterward, from prison, he would write: "Doing doubles is far more difficult than doing singles, but on the other hand it also puts one in a position to have twice as much fun. There can be some lively discussions about which of the victims will get to be killed first. When you have a pair of teenaged bimbolinas bound hand and foot and ready for a session with the skinning knife, neither one of the little devils wants to be the one to go first. And they don't mind telling you quickly why their best friend should be the one to die."

Today, authorities suggest the Hangman's first "doubles" were 21-year-old Nancy Leichner and 20-year-old Pamela Ann Nater, casual acquaintances who went on a picnic with the "Aquaholics" scuba diving club at the Ocala National Forest's Alexander Springs Recreation Area in Altoona, Florida, on October 2, 1966. The petite, attractive girls—one blonde, the other brunette—were accompanied by Leichner's fiancé and Nater's steady boyfriend, but they were last seen walking off together, unaccompanied, entering the woods on one of the site's nature trails. Behind them, on a picnic table, they'd left their street clothes and shoes, their purses, Leichner's eyeglasses and other personal items. Searchers fanned out over 15 square miles when the women failed to return, but no trace of them has been found to this day. Polygraph tests cleared their male companions of any suspicion, and police noted that the women had met only one time before they went missing, ruling out any motive for an orchestrated disappearance. Three decades after they vanished, investigators declared themselves "certain" that Schaefer abducted and murdered both women.

Mike McGonigle saw no indication that his friend from high school was a murderer when they met up in summer 1967. "We went camping in Ontario for two weeks," he told the *Miami Herald.* "John would spend all the time he could hunting and fishing. He really loved the Everglades. It made us both mad to see all this development going on. We used to be able to hunt west of Hollywood Boulevard."

An environmentally conscious Hangman? Or simply one concerned about where to dump fresh bodies next?

*****

In January 1968, Schaefer enrolled at Florida Atlantic University in Boca Raton, seeking a teacher's certificate. Cut off from the priesthood and washed out of Up With People, he saw education as the next best way to mold young minds. Residing in a dormitory for the first time, he was pleased to find Jerry Webster, a friend from 1962, living down the hall. While out of touch for several years, Webster recalled, "We both liked hunting, fishing, [and] English literature." While living in the dorm, Schaefer submitted stories to various fiction magazines, recounting his outdoor adventures, but none were published.

The war in Vietnam was going badly for America in early 1968, thanks to the January Tet Offensive that came close to overwhelming troops at Hué, Khe Sanh, and even in Saigon. At home, the draft was ramping up, and by April, Schaefer's lackluster grades no longer supported a student deferment. Once allegedly gung-ho to join the Army and "kill things," he'd changed his mind over the past three years and dreaded being posted in harm's way. That month, when ordered to report for his induction physical, the Hangman left a suicide note in his dorm room and fled.

Jerry Webster, seemingly naïve, later told the *Miami Herald,* "John was a very personable, nonviolent kind of person who objected strenuously to violence. When they called me and told me he left a suicide note, I drove out that night to where we used to practice target shooting and found John target shooting. He did it to help him get the deferment. He was already seeing a psychiatrist to help him stay out of the Army."

Decades later, Schaefer and his medical records told a rather different story. On May 20, 1968, Dr. Raymond Killinger, FAU's resident psychiatrist, referred Schaefer to the Florida University Testing and Evaluation Center "for psychological evaluation on an emergency basis." Psychometrist R. R. McCormick sat with Schaefer for two hours and thirty minutes, reporting "excellent" rapport and test results "prolific in psycho-dynamic information." McCormick found that Schaefer "is immature, has poor ego control, is aggressive and rebellious and primarily has an intense father conflict. In addition, his personality dynamics incline him to blame others for his own difficulties. He is extremely confused in terms of self-image and is alienated from himself and others." McCormick noted "decreased ego control and impairment in reality testing that is often found among psychotics or individuals with intra-cranial [*sic*] pathology." At the end of their meeting, Schaefer said, "I feel fine but at times I feel different—like it isn't real. Not like I black out, but things just go."

Decades later, through letters placed in evidence with a federal court, Schaefer treated the whole episode as a humorous scam. He wrote: "I got drafted. I got down to the point to be sworn in, and in my best thespian manner, asked if it was gonna be OK to be in the army if I'm queer? ...Fastest dismissal you ever did see. Oh, they interrogate you but the key is to be sincere...Of *course* I want to be in the army, I just wondered if there was any rule against wearing panties? Threw me right out the door."

Schaefer also claimed he supported the fraud by attending classes in nylons and a garter belt. Oddly, no classmates from FAU recall him ever turning up in drag. Tellingly, that version of events only surfaced in 1973, when homicide detectives found photos of a "male figure" clad in lingerie among the many items seized from Doris Schaefer's home.

*****

Dodging Vietnam was relatively simple, but Schaefer's long war on the homefront continued. Gerard Sr. lost his job with Kimberly-Clark in May 1968 and sought solace with a mistress, bringing her home to meet his wife in July, whereupon Doris filed for divorce, charging Gerard Sr. with adultery and habitual drunkenness. Seething, the Hangman quit his summer construction job and embarked on a hunting trip to Michigan, later claiming he spent August in Chicago "with a cadre from SDS"—the radically anti-war Students for a Democratic

Society who joined Black Panthers, "Yippies," and others for riotous protests at the Democratic National Convention, held that month in the Windy City.

Wherever Schaefer actually spent his summer, he returned to Florida accompanied by Marty Fogg, his near-miss paramour from Sing Out '66 and now his fiancée. According to Mike McGonigle, "He met up with Marty somewhere in Michigan while he was traveling. When he told me he was engaged, I told him he was crazy. He had only known her for a few weeks."

Jerry Webster held a similar view. "Marty was a genius," he told the *Herald.* "John is very intelligent, but he is a very competitive person, and it was hard for him to be with a genius like Marty." Nonetheless, they married in December 1968, with McGonigle serving as best man. Schaefer returned the favor when McGonigle wed his own fiancée 10 months later. Meanwhile, the Hangman and Marty moved in with Doris Schaefer, while Gerard pursued his goal of becoming a teacher. To that end, Schaefer attended FAU in spring 1969, then both FAU and BCC in autumn of that year. Marty enrolled at BCC and worked part-time at Port Everglades.

Briefly, they presented a façade of wedded bliss, but it was not to last.

On his first student-teaching application, Schaefer wrote, "I believe that the teacher should strive to reflect and preserve the attitudes and standards of the community in which he teaches since his actions are influential to the children in his charge." Jerry Webster put it another way, to the *Herald*: "John had very strong opinions and he wanted people to know his opinions."

It didn't wash at Plantation High School, where Schaefer served his first stint as an intern in the social sciences department. He lasted only a few weeks before the school canned him for "trying to impose his moral and political views on his students." Principal Bill Haines termed Schaefer's behavior "totally inappropriate."

That winter tested Schaefer's marriage. He was jobless, living now with Marty in their own apartment, but as Mike McGonigle's wife told reporters, "He couldn't care less. He went hunting and fishing all the time. He wasn't mature about it. He wasn't responsible."

Unknown to Marty and the McGonigles, the Hangman was killing again.

*****

Schaefer's parents finally divorced in September 1969 as their eldest son returned to Florida Atlantic University. Three days after classes started, a mysterious fate overtook an ex-neighbor, once the object of Gerard's teenage lust and self-righteous fury.

Leigh Hainline, 25, married Charles Bonadies on August 21, 1969, but their union—

31

like Schaefer's with Marty—soon dissolved into constant arguing. One bone of contention was Leigh's claim that childhood neighbor and sometime tennis partner Gerard Schaefer had offered her a job with the Central Intelligence Agency, starting at $20,000 per year. Charles scoffed at the idea of Leigh becoming a secret agent and told her to forget it. On September 8, he came home from work to an empty apartment and a note from Leigh, saying she'd left for Miami. She never returned, and police found her car abandoned in a Fort Lauderdale parking lot.

Leigh's family hired a private detective to find her, and Schaefer spoke to the investigator. He denied any knowledge of the CIA or Leigh's whereabouts, but in a later conversation with Leigh's brother, Gary—a friend from junior high school, home on leave from the army—Schaefer claimed Leigh had called him before leaving home, asking him for a ride to the airport. She was flying out to Cincinnati, Leigh allegedly explained, and promised to call Schaefer back with a flight departure time, but that was the last he'd heard from her. Her name did not appear on any flight's passenger list. Charles filed for divorce on October 6, and a court granted his petition on March 10, 1970. Another eight years passed before Leigh's bullet-punctured skull surfaced at Boca Del Mar.

*****

Schaefer took another stab at student teaching in autumn 1969, placed this time by FAU administrators at Stranahan High School in Fort Lauderdale. He had apparently learned nothing from the first go-round, and following a series of political harangues in his class on "Americanism vs. Communism," supervisor Richard Goodhart removed him on November 11. This time, the verdict went beyond rejection. As Goodhart later informed reporters, "I told him when he left that he'd better never let me hear of his trying to get a job with any authority over other people, or I'd do anything I could to see that he didn't get it." Four years later, Schaefer blamed the school, telling psychiatrists, "They only wanted black people."

Schaefer withdrew from FAU again, this time blaming marital problems. For a change, it was closer to the truth than most of his excuses. After 11 months, his marriage was failing, though another half-year would pass before Marty filed for divorce, citing Gerard for "extreme cruelty."

The Hangman claimed his next known victim in December 1969, just a month after he blew his second teaching gig. The victim was 22-year-old Carmen Marie Hallock, nicknamed "Candy," a cocktail waitress who earned enough working nights to enroll as a full-time student at Broward Community College. She also briefly dated Jack Dolan. Lunching with ex-sister-in-law Nancy Bauer on December 18, Hallock

33

mentioned a date she had that evening, with "a teacher" from BCC. Aside from teaching, he allegedly visited the Bahamas most weekends, returning with "lots of money." Better yet, he'd offered Hallock some kind of "undercover" work that featured an apartment in Manhattan or Washington, D.C., with all expenses paid. Hallock seemed upbeat when she left work that night, last seen alive by a bartender friend at the Brave Bull saloon on North Federal Highway. She wore a black chiffon dress and matching shoes. From there, she drove home to her apartment on Fort Lauderdale's Sunrise Boulevard, drew a bath—and vanished.

Come Christmas Day, without a word from Hallock, Nancy Bauer used a spare key to enter Carmen's apartment. She found Hallock's puppy, apparently unfed for days, and noted the bathtub filled with water, unused and long since cold. Looking around, Bauer noted that Hallock's car keys and driver's license were missing, along with the black dress and shoes she'd been wearing when last seen alive. A few days later, police found Hallock's car abandoned at English Park, not far from home.

Candy had stepped into a fog of mystery resembling that which had enveloped Leigh Bonadies three months earlier, complete with tales of international intrigue. Homicide detectives got their first clue to her fate in April 1973.

*****

In March 1970, Schaefer petitioned FAU administrators to alter his records, changing his November 1969 withdrawal to an "incomplete," thereby readmitting him as a full-time student. They agreed, and Marty briefly joined him on campus, but their union was doomed. She filed for divorce on May 2, and Schaefer failed to contest it, a pattern he would replicate twice more in future years.

Perhaps the Hangman was relieved to be alone again.

Schaefer rebounded from the break-up with a month-long summer trip to Europe and North Africa, including a ride on the Marrakesh Express, a Moroccan railroad popularized in 1969 by singers Crosby, Stills, Nash and Young. He would later boast of victims murdered on "three continents," and while this journey might account for some, no homicides outside of the United States have been confirmed.

Back at FAU that fall, Schaefer supported himself as a watchman for Florida Light and Power, employed by Wackenhut Security of Coral Gables (now G4S Secure Solutions). He rented a house in Osceola Village, off State Road 84, sharing the digs with former Saint Thomas Aquinas classmate Jack Dolan. Questioned later by Schaefer's defense attorney, Dolan recalled the house as "really old," decrepit, and smelling "like a kennel" thanks to Schaefer's ever-drooling dog. "I couldn't wait to get out of there," Dolan said. "I was completely disgusted and a little bit scared. John was just getting a little bit weird."

As an example of that "weirdness," Dolan told the lawyer Schaefer had shown him snapshots from his summer abroad, then said, "I've got some other pictures too." When Dolan asked to see them, Schaefer chuckled and replied, "You don't want to see those pictures." Three years later, homicide detectives would collect them in a search of Doris Schaefer's home. By then, the Hangman would be using Dolan as a scapegoat for some of his crimes.

*****

On December 29, 1970, two Pompano Beach girls—nine-year-old blonde Peggy Rahn and eight-year-old brunette Wendy Brown Stevenson —met up at their hometown's famous seashore. Both attended Palmview Elementary School, but while they had mutual friends, they hadn't met before their last known day alive. They arrived at the beach separately, Peggy brought by a family friend, while Wendy's uncle accompanied her, but the girls left their adult escorts at 1:00 p.m., walking to an ice cream stand in the parking lot. Neither was ever seen again.

Police in such a case start with the most obvious suspects, but polygraph tests cleared Wendy's uncle and Peggy's adult friend. Alerted by publicity, on December 30 a clerk at a nearby convenience store reported a man buying ice cream for two young girls the previous afternoon. The clerk identified photos of Peggy and Wendy, describing their companion as white, 25 to 30 years old, sandy-haired, around six feet tall and weighing 190 to 200 pounds. He'd worn a gray pinstriped sport coat over a red turtleneck and blue jeans. The clerk identified his car as a metallic blue 1966 or '67 Chevrolet with a vinyl top and wire wheels, license number unknown.

Suspicion next fell on Kenneth Guy Shilts, a Michigan native and serial child molester arrested in Alabama six weeks after the Florida girls disappeared. Shilts carried a notebook allegedly recording his assaults in primitive code, including the entry "Peggy and Wendy— Pompano Beach." He also admitted being in central Florida on December 29 but denied abducting the two missing girls. That said, officers could find no hard evidence linking Shilts to the case, and he died in 1991 without being charged.

In 1973, Florida prosecutors publicly accused Schaefer of snatching the girls, and while he denied it publicly, a private letter penned 16 years later admitted roasting and cannibalizing both victims.

True or false? The case remains officially unsolved.

*****

Standing guard at Florida Light and Power had one sweet fringe benefit: Schaefer's meeting with secretary Teresa Dolly Dean, seven years his junior. They began dating while he continued study at FAU, now working toward a bachelor's degree in geography. He reached that goal in August 1971 and celebrated by marrying Teresa on September 11.

Alas, Schaefer's new geography degree was useless without a teaching credential, and that door, like the priesthood, was now permanently closed to him. What other job would possibly permit him to root out and cure the brooding evils of society?

It came to Schaefer in a flash.

He would become a cop.

Chapter 3: Lawman

By 1971, Gerard Schaefer had failed once at marriage, washed out of the priesthood, and was barred from teaching. If we believe his own account, he'd also stopped writing graphic tales of murder as a form of doctor-ordered psychological release and had stashed the manuscripts at his mother's house in Fort Lauderdale. He was adrift, skeet shooting as a hobby, allegedly becoming "number two in the state," while he cast about for prospective employment. What was a newly remarried man to do, with his eternal quest to "put things right" in a corrupt society?

What else, indeed, but don a uniform and badge?

Murders aside, he still faced certain obstacles. Within two years, he would admit to suffering from diabetes and "a touch of gout" but claimed to keep both illnesses in check by means of diet. Known from ancient Egypt onward as "the disease of kings," gout occurs primarily in overweight patients who consume large quantities of meat and beer (rarely available to peasants during olden times), producing inflammatory arthritis (often in the feet) and abnormal levels of uric acid in the blood. Today, dietary regulations and regular doses of vitamin C often hold the disease in abeyance.

Health issues aside, there remained the matter of proper training at Broward Community College's police academy program, a 22-week regimen consisting of eight hour days, five days per week, designed, in the school's own words, "to prepare a student for the physical and mental demands of a career as a Florida police officer or deputy sheriff." The drawback: first, enrollees must be hired and sponsored by some certified law enforcement agency.

Schaefer tried the Broward County Sheriff's Office first, but failed the department's preliminary psychological examination for undisclosed reasons, earning an outright rejection. His next stop: Wilton Manors, 12 miles north of Fort Lauderdale and bordering on Oakland Park. Police Chief Bernard Scott—an ex-welder with 13 years in uniform and five as head of the city's 26-member department, riding herd on 10,948 residents—hired Schaefer in late August 1971, unaware of his glitch with the BCSO psych exam. In September, Schaefer entered the police academy's basic recruit certification program, emerging as a probationary officer in January 1972.

*****

Blonde Belinda Hutchins (or Hutchens, in some accounts) was a 22-year-old wife and mother, living with mechanic husband William in Fort

40

Lauderdale and working as a cocktail waitress when Schaefer earned his badge. She had an eye for easy money and was nabbed in a November 1970 prostitution sting, by cops posing as "johns," paying a $252 fine.

That was Belinda's sole arrest, but sources claim she flaunted extramarital affairs, while William grappled with "drug problems." On the night of January 4, 1972, Belinda's husband and their two-year-old daughter watched her climb into a light-blue Datsun sedan and drive away, never to be seen again. William reported Belinda missing on Wednesday, January 5, but the search went nowhere, even with the costly aid of a private detective. Eighteen months later, *Inside Detective* claimed that Belinda "kept a diary containing the names of many men, some of which would be recognized if made public." One name that meant nothing to police or Belinda's family in January 1972 was "Jerry Sheppard." Only in May 1973, when shown the Hangman's blue Datsun, would William Hutchins declare, "That's the car."

*****

Eight weeks after Belinda Hutchins's vanishing act, on February 29, 13-year-old Debora Sue Lowe disappeared while walking the mile from her home in Pompano Beach to Rickards Middle School, at 8th Street and Sunrise Boulevard.

41

When last seen, she wore a tan poncho over a yellow blouse and black slacks with vertical rose-colored stripes. When she failed to report for class, administrators phoned her home and a search began. Police initially believed that she had run away, perhaps returning to Palestine, West Virginia, where her family had lived until recently. Debora's parents rejected that idea, noting that none of her treasured belongings were missing, and in any case, she never made it back to Palestine, 1,025 miles north of Pompano Beach.

Subsequent investigation revealed that Gerard Schaefer once worked with Debora's father and had visited her home numerous times, while the Lowes also attended cookouts at Schaefer's place on several occasions. Forty-five years after the fact, Debora remains a missing person, but her family is convinced that Schaefer snatched and murdered her.

*****

While females vanished in South Florida, probationary officer Gerard Schaefer was working the not-so-mean streets of Wilton Manors—and he had trouble almost from the start. Chief Scott would later say his new man didn't have "an ounce of common sense. He used poor judgment, did dumb things." As one example, Scott cited a day when Schaefer was assigned to work the scene of a traffic collision. While the sergeant in charge questioned witnesses, Schaefer's job was directing traffic, but his supervisor soon found him lounging against a streetlamp, snacking on potato chips.

Fellow officers reportedly complained that Schaefer was "badge-heavy," throwing his weight around on the job, though Chief Scott denied it. According to FBI profiler Robert Ressler, the problem went further than that. In his book *Whoever Fights Monsters* (1992), Ressler wrote: "According to my conversations with officers connected to the case, in his earlier job [Wilton Manors P.D.], Schaefer had been cited for stopping cars driven by women committing traffic infractions, then running the women's license plate numbers through a computer check to obtain more particulars about them, and getting their phone numbers so he could call them later for dates."

If true, Chief Scott never acknowledged such activities when questioned after Schaefer's final fall from grace, nor would Schaefer confess to cheating on wife Teresa with strangers. But author Sondra London—formerly Schaefer's high school sweetheart Sandy Stewart—writes of "a female motorist in a white car passing through Wilton Manors while Schaefer was employed there as a police officer. After being stopped by a police officer, the woman disappeared." Oddly, London says "no police reports document her identity," thus making the alleged crime impossible to trace, but she wrote in 1997 that "the case is still talked about by old-timers in law enforcement circles."

Another unknown victim of the Hangman?

With or without missing women, by spring 1972, Chief Scott had seen enough of Schaefer. "I didn't want him around," he later told reporters, and he had slated Gerard for summary dismissal before completion of his probationary period when Schaefer surprised him, winning a commendation for his role in a drug bust. The incident saved Schaefer's job, but only briefly. Within days he was back to his old tricks, and Chief Scott called him in for a final showdown on April 19. Teary-eyed, Schaefer begged for an umpteenth chance to improve, and Scott relented.

One day later, though, other police departments started calling Scott, reporting Schaefer's attempts to join their agencies. Furious, Scott cut him loose, barely eight months after hiring Schaefer and sending him to the police academy. As for the departments seeking a recommendation, Chief Scott recalled, "I told them I would put on a uniform and walk the streets myself before I would have him back."

*****

Schaefer had burned his bridges in Broward County, so he cast his eyes northward to Martin County, on the Treasure Coast. Sprawling over 753 square miles, Martin County harbored a population of 28,035 in 1970's census, encompassing the 1,035-acre Hobe Sound National Wildlife Refuge and other wilderness areas of the kind Schaefer had long enjoyed. Best of all, Governor Reuben Askew had lately appointed Sheriff Robert L. Crowder—only one year Schaefer's senior, at 27—to replace late 20-year incumbent Roy Baker. Schaefer applied for a deputy's job, bolstered by a glowing letter of recommendation bearing Chief Scott's forged signature, and Sheriff Crowder hired him on June 30 without any background investigation.

That was a mistake he would regret within three weeks, but in the meantime Schaefer and Teresa pulled up stakes in Broward County, moving to the Martin County seat at Stuart, population at the time 4,820. Schaefer donned his new badge and uniform, settling into what he hoped would be the true beginning of his new career.

If only he could hold his private demons at bay.

*****

Pamela Sue Wells and Nancy Ellen Trotter were strangers when they met in Stuart, Florida, on

July 20, 1972, but they might have been peas in a pod. Both were attractive teenagers, aged 18 and 17 respectively, who'd come to Florida seeking summer sunshine, Wells hailing from Texas, while Trotter came from Illinois. They'd bonded quickly, instant friends, and on July 21 they hitched a ride together, bikini clad, to popular Jensen beach. After a few hours sunning themselves and fending off amorous boys, they were thumbing their way back to Stuart when the Hangman entered their lives.

Schaefer was driving his patrol car, clad in uniform, when he pulled up and asked the girls where they were going. Telling them falsely that it was illegal to hitchhike in Martin County, Schaefer radioed headquarters and asked permission to drive the girls back to their rented lodgings. Approval came at once.

En route to Stuart, Schaefer introduced himself by his real name—perhaps because he knew they'd seen the name tag on his shirt—and asked if they would like a lift next morning, back to Jensen Beach. The beach was part of his patrol route, Schaefer said, and so the girls agreed, suspecting nothing out of place.

On July 21, Schaefer met Trotter and Wells at Memorial Park, next door to Martin County's courthouse. Instead of yesterday's patrol car, he drove a light-blue Datsun, clad in a civilian shirt and slacks, explaining that he had been "temporarily assigned" to plainclothes duty.

That made sense to Wells and Trotter, who wore swimsuits underneath their shirts and jeans. With Nancy in the front seat, Sue in back, they drove away on Highway A1A, also called Southeast Ocean Boulevard.

Instead of driving straight to Jensen Beach, Schaefer asked if his passengers would like to see an ancient Spanish fort up close. They both agreed, and Schaefer drove them across the Indian River onto Hutchinson Island, a narrow barrier island stretching 23 miles from north to south. Martin County claims the southern one-third of Hutchinson Island, limiting construction on the unincorporated area and preserving much of it for wildlife, including service as a nesting ground for endangered sea turtles. The northern two-thirds, owned by St. Lucie County, features tourist motels, golfing, sailing and surfing, among other draws for vacationing outsiders.

Once on Hutchinson, the Hangman drove his teenage guests to a dilapidated building with a long-neglected dock, which he called the "Spanish fort." The girls stepped out to look around, but didn't want to linger. Put off by the locale, mosquitoes, and their yen for the beach, they soon piled back into Schaefer's Datsun—where the interrogation began.

"He started asking us questions," Nancy later told reporters, vaguely referring to a "halfway house" run by "Jesus freaks," one of whom had allegedly shared her apartment with

Trotter and Wells. Next, he asked "if there were drugs there," which both girls swiftly denied. Casting a broader net, he asked them next, "Where are the drugs in Stuart?" Wells and Trotter both pled ignorance, explaining that they'd only been in town two days. Next came "a whole bunch of questions," disjointed and vague, while they sat in Schaefer's car. The girls tried to maintain their equanimity, but Schaefer's monologue soon took a darker turn.

"He told us he could dig a hole and bury us," Trotter recalled, adding, "No crime without a victim. We still didn't think he was serious. We were just getting disgusted, because it was hot and we wanted to get to the beach."

Some of the jocularity deserted Schaefer's tone as he ordered both girls from the car, saying that they were under arrest as runaways. Wells retorted that her parents knew where she was, and it made no difference anyway, since she was 18. Undeterred, Schaefer reached between the Datsun's bucket seats, grabbed two pairs of handcuffs and secured each captive's hands behind her back. As Trotter described it, he next asked, "Would your parents pay ransom?" From there, Schaefer's monologue leapt to "a bunch of weird stuff" about white slavery. Specifically, Trotter reported, "He said he had someone he could sell us to, and then he could really see the world. We told him to go get his sheik and sell us.

He was mad because we wouldn't talk to him and weren't scared."

Not, that is, until Schaefer opened the Datsun's trunk and removed a blanket, which he spread on the ground. Next came "ropes and sheets," some of which he used to gag his captives. He separated the girls, first warning both that if either tried to escape, he would kill the one nearest to him, then run down and slay the other. Each in turn was taken to a tree and balanced on a root with ankles bound, hands still cuffed at their backs, before the Hangman rigged a noose around each victim's neck and tied it to an overhanging limb. Balance was critical, since if their feet slipped from the gnarled perches, they would slowly and inevitably strangle.

That accomplished, Schaefer suddenly surprised his captives, saying that he had to leave and fetch "a friend," but promising he would return soon and complete whatever twisted scheme he had in mind. In fact, he'd realized that he would soon be late for roll call at the sheriff's office. Afterward, there would be ample time to double back and finish off his prey.

*****

Stories of how the prisoners escaped vary among published accounts. The most elaborate, published by *True Detective* in October 1973, claims Schaefer led Trotter to a site at the edge of the Indian River before he placed her in position to be hanged by accident unless she kept her balance under stress. "I was crying," she said, "but the only thing he really did to me was pinch my bottom. I got a kind of disgusted look on my face and he laughed. He made some statement that if he wanted to, he could have raped me right there."

Schaefer left her then and, as she told the magazine, Trotter immediately tried to free herself, slumping against the tree trunk that supported her. She chewed her gag to loosen it, then somehow shed her noose, even with hands still cuffed behind her back. (Other reports claim Trotter was still gagged when found, and offer no coherent explanation as to how she slipped the noose from off her neck.) Unable to see Pamela or their kidnapper, *True Detective* quoted Trotter's claims that she next hid the ropes from which she had escaped, aware from glimpsing Schaefer's open auto trunk that he had no more stashed inside.

In Trotter's version of the tale, she "sneaked behind the Spanish fort and peeked out the other side," immediately spotting Schaefer's car. She ran back toward the river then and waded in knee-deep before she thought she heard a voice calling her name. Peering through some brush, she saw Wells in the same position Schaefer had left Nancy in, suspended from another tree, but had no view of Schaefer himself. Sounds "like

50

someone was behind me" drove her farther out into the water, finally swimming awkwardly when it became too deep to wade, stung twice by jellyfish before she reached dry land again and stumbled on to Highway A1A, where Sheriff Crowder's cruiser soon appeared.

A month before that story went to press, *Inside Detective* spun a different tale. The girls had been strung up together, according to author Vernon Bill, and managed to escape simultaneously when Schaefer left them to attend the standard roll call for his shift. Together, "still handcuffed and gagged, they began making their way back to the highway." Nonetheless, they had been separated on their trek, and Sheriff Crowder found Trotter first, then sent a sidekick, one Lieutenant Waldron, to find Wells "back there" in the tangled forest.

The whole escape, however it progressed in fact, consumed about three-quarters of an hour by the victims' estimates. It seems like a bizarre coincidence that they would meet Schaefer's employer on the highway after they untied themselves and crossed the river, but in fact the Hangman brought it on himself.

After roll call, Schaefer drove back to his would-be murder site and found his prisoners had fled. Panicked, since he had given them his real name, Schaefer called headquarters, hoping he could bluff it out with his new boss. When Sheriff Crowder took the call, Schaefer began, "You're going to be mad at me. I've done something foolish." As he told the tale, he'd "overdone" his job, trying to "scare" two girls out of future hitchhiking "for their own good." It was a "dumb mistake," the Hangman granted, although well intentioned.

Sheriff Crowder kept his cool on the phone, ordering Schaefer back to headquarters. Perhaps the county's newest deputy believed he had a chance to save himself, but he was wrong. When Schaefer reached the sheriff's office, Crowder fired him instantly, informing him of Crowder's plan to charge him with two counts of false imprisonment, plus two more of aggravated assault. Schaefer's formal booking photo as prisoner No. 4390, dated two days after the botched abduction, still reveals what seems to be an enigmatic grin. He posted $15,000 bail and went home to Teresa, free until his scheduled trial in November.

The Schaefer scandal was a grave humiliation to Sheriff Crowder, amplified when he belatedly checked out the Hangman's reference from Wilton Manors, only to discover it was forged. Despite seeming inept, Crowder tried to make the best of it at a press conference four days later, branding Schaefer's crime "a great embarrassment to anyone in law enforcement. It could not have been foreseen from earlier contact with the man." He finished up, telling reporters, "Guess we had one bad apple in the bunch."

Candidate James D. Holt won the 1972 sheriff's election, serving for the next two decades, but Crowder rebounded in 1992, reclaiming his former office and holding it until 2013.

Meanwhile, unknown to Schaefer, he had witnessed the beginning of the end. But he was not caged yet. While he marked time until his day in court, more hapless victims waited to be claimed.

Chapter 4: Busted

If anyone supposed the Hangman would behave himself while free on bond, they were gravely mistaken. Of course, few dealing with him in the weeks after his "foolish" act with two victims who got away had any clue as to the morbid obsession controlling his life. He hunted girls and women down because he *wanted* to, because it *pleased* him, satisfying something in the black void a naïve priest might have called his soul.

The Hangman's course was set, had been for years. He could no more resist the urges simmering within him than an unmanned drone aircraft, directed from a secret hangar somewhere in America's Southwest, could disobey its orders to attack and kill targets inside Iraq, Afghanistan, or any other distant nation which the White House and the Pentagon deem "hostile."

Schaefer was on a roll, and while he was at liberty, the dice were hot.

The end would come, in its own time, but that would not spare other innocents.

*****

Before he struck again, however, while biding his time between release on bond and his November trial, Schaefer appeared normal in all respects—

donning what psychiatrist Hervey Milton Cleckley had dubbed the psychopath's "mask of sanity" in his 1941 book of the same title. Schaefer's arrest and impending conviction made it difficult for him to find a job, but he worked briefly in two different grocery stores and, ironically, as an apprentice meat cutter. He also took Teresa on a week-long road trip to Colorado and back, then made one of his frequent hunting excursions to the Dakotas, accompanied by Teresa and another Fort Lauderdale couple. No record survives of whatever he killed on that jaunt, but his mind was back in Florida, anticipating further human prey.

*****

Susan Place and Georgia Marie Jessup were newly minted friends in September 1972. One year apart in age—Susan was 17, Georgia 16—they met in classes at Oakland Park's Downtown Education Center where both were making up lost high school credits. Susan's grades were lagging, and Georgia had dropped out entirely, despite scoring A's and B's. Her mother, Shirley, said, "She kept losing her place in school. She was always searching for something, but she didn't know what."

Aside from spotty academic skills, the girls also shared a love of music, lounging on Florida's beaches, albeit at different times, and hanging out with quasi-hippie types who whiled away their days and nights at Captain Kidd's, a burger joint where idle youths mingled with tourists on the go. In the spirit of the time, Georgia preferred the nickname "Crystal." Unlike Place, her parents were divorced. She lived with father George in an apartment six miles from mother Shirley's second-story flat, thus shortening her trip to school.

Georgia's parents remember her as "a peace and love girl," but "an average teenager" nonetheless. Shirley Jessup told reporters, "The world was her oyster and she wanted to change it. She just wasn't satisfied with the world. The war [in Vietnam] bothered her." Susan, by contrast, "lived for music" in the words of her mother, Lucille. She played piano and guitar while writing poetry that sometimes lent itself to song. She also had a secret: epilepsy, which she managed to control with medication and conceal from most acquaintances. In early childhood, a severe attack left Susan partially paralyzed on her right side, whereupon she'd learned to write and play guitar with her left hand.

Both girls were open to new friendships and discussed a life of ease, out on the open road. Both were also attractive—Susan blonde, Georgia brunette. Shirley Jessup recalled that Georgia "always had lots of boys bugging her. She wasn't exactly a teaser, but she told the boys to keep their hands off." Susan's smile could light up any room.

Enter the Hangman.

Georgia met him first, as homicide detectives later reconstructed the event. The circumstances of their first encounter are unknown, leaving authorities to speculate. One night, he came to George Jessup's door and asked for Crystal. Georgia's father later said, "I told him there was no Crystal here. You're probably talking about Georgia Jessup." The visitor agreed, and introduced himself as "Jerry Shepherd." He described himself to George as "an outdoorsman," adding that "he had been in the mountains of Colorado and places like that." George judged the man to be some 11 years Georgia's senior, around 27 years old.

In retrospect, George Jessup knew little of when or where his daughter met Shepherd. He told the *Palm Beach Post-Times* (which dropped the *Times* in 1979) that she had "mentioned him" in passing, but George then contradicted himself, quoting Georgia as saying she'd met Shepherd "a long time ago and they were renewing their acquaintance." Shirley Jessup cast that statement in a different light, telling the *Post-Times*, "It was one of those psychic things. She believed in reincarnation and she felt she knew him." George was surprised when Georgia mentioned that she might be joining Shepherd on a trip to Colorado, visiting friends of his at an unspecified state university.

Once they'd conferred, too late, the parents of both girls suspected their daughters had met Shepherd recently, in mid-September, around the time the girls became acquainted with each other at the Downtown Education Center. How they met remained anyone's guess.

Lucille Place noted that her daughter shared a sense of wanderlust with Georgia Jessup. Susan missed the family's former home in Royal Oak, a suburb of Detroit, and stuck close to her older sister, Kristen, helping her run a Beatles Fan Club from their home, later expanding her musical horizon to include Led Zeppelin. Like Georgia, Susan was a "peace and love" girl who "didn't down the hippies. She thought they were people too," Lucille told the *Post-Times*. Susan "didn't date much," but rather "liked to be with a lot of people." When Susan craved a nighttime visit to the beach, her parents drove and waited for her while she walked along the sand. "I told her to don't ever hitchhike," Lucille said. "You're liable to find yourself in a ditch."

Prophetic words.

On Wednesday night, September 27, Shirley Jessup left work and let herself into ex-husband George's apartment, looking forward to an amicable family dinner. George was out, and Shirley found a note from Georgia. It read: "I'm sorry, Mother and Dad. I love you both very much. I have to find my head." A quick look around showed that Georgia's suitcase and various personal items were gone.

The Hangman had appeared in George's absence and before Shirley arrived. His next stop was the Place home, where Susan's family knew him only by reputation. Around the same time Georgia warned her father that she might be joining Shepherd on a trip out west, Susan advised her family that she'd considered joining Georgia and Shepherd on the drive to Colorado. Arriving with Georgia on September 27, Shepherd introduced himself to Susan's family, smiling and nodding along as Susan said, "We're just going to the beach to play guitar." Lucille Place warned Shepherd that Susan required medication to thwart epileptic seizures, but the pills remained forgotten in a dresser drawer. Lucille, who considered herself "a bit psychic," felt Shepherd seemed "too nice" and made note of the license plate on his blue-green Datsun, unconsciously omitting one of its first two numbers. She also glanced into the car, glimpsing a white Styrofoam cooler on the backseat. "I really wanted to look inside," she later said, "but I didn't."

Susan failed to return that night, and again on Thursday. Recalling her daughter's mention of Colorado, Ira and Lucille Place bided their time, allowing three more days to pass before concern morphed into fear. Before calling police, Lucille thought of Georgia, aka Crystal, but didn't know her last name. A mutual friend, Jan Snyder, supplied it, and Lucille phoned George Jessup on Sunday, October 1, learning that Georgia had apparently run off from home.

Lucille's next call went to the Oakland Park Police Department on North Dixie Highway. As she later explained to the *Post-Times,* "I told them the man's name was Shepherd, and I even gave them the license number of the car. I handed them all this information on a silver platter, and they wouldn't even investigate." Shirley Jessup, meanwhile, had called the Broward County Sheriff's Department the same night she found Georgia's note. "They just didn't want to be bothered," she told reporters. "They wouldn't do anything. In fact, one of them told me, 'Oh, they're probably just shacking up somewhere'."

Dissatisfied, both sets of parents soon adopted a routine, driving along the highways fronting local beaches, searching for their missing girls. They failed, and Susan's eighteenth birthday passed without a celebration on October 4. Instead, Lucille Place learned to live with grim, disturbing dreams. In one, she told the *Post-Times,* "Susan was in a corner with her hand over her mouth. She removed her hand and it was bloody. All her teeth were gone." In another dream, Susan had told Lucille, "I'm going to come home, Mother," but would not answer when Lucille begged, "Sue, just let me know where you are." After each dream, Lucille told the *Post-Times*, "I would read in the newspapers of another body being found somewhere in the state."

But none of them belonged to Susan or her missing friend.

Not yet.

*****

Several days after Jessup and Place disappeared, Georgia's father found a letter marked "Return to Sender" in his mailbox. It was addressed to Jerry Shepherd, at a post office box in Daytona Beach and was returned because Shepherd had closed the box in July 1972—soon after Schaefer posted bond in the Martin County case of victims Nancy Trotter and Pamela Wells. Despite closing the box, Schaefer—as Shepherd—apparently still used it in conversation as a possible contact address.

Opening the returned envelope, George Jessup found a letter his missing daughter had written to Shepherd. It read, in part:

> I'm very lonely where I live because there's no one I could talk to. I wish some of my friends would move over to this neighborhood. You know something, remember you said when we met it was like we were

61

old friends meeting again. Well, it was that way. Maybe you were a friend of mine in a former life. It's not impossible, you know.

I have a tent. I only wish I could use it but dad would never agree to let me go camping by myself. Oh, well, at least I can dream. Please write to me.

No answer ever came from Schaefer, sitting in the Martin County jail.

*****

On October 23, 18 days after Place and Jessup disappeared from Oakland Park, two 14-year-old friends—Mary Alice Briscolina and Elsie Lina Farmer—vanished from Pompano Beach. The girls, both residents of Coral Ridge Isles, north of Fort Lauderdale, were polar opposites in looks. *Inside Detective* called Mary "a budding beauty, raven-haired with an olive complexion and a ripening figure." She was also a late-life baby, both her parents over 40, who sometimes locked herself in her bedroom until boys came calling for dates. Even so, Mrs. Briscolina told reporters, "Mary was a good girl, and any time one of those boys went too far, she'd let them know about it."

Elsie, on the other hand, was shorter, heavyset, self-conscious and shy, a child of divorce who lived with a half-brother and drew no attention from boys. Nonetheless, at an age when high school students grow painfully aware of looks, style, and appeals to the "in-crowd," Mary and Elsie bonded as friends. Both girls shared the wanderlust of Susan Place and Georgia Jessup, prone to hitchhiking and skimping on details when asked where they'd gone. Mary's mother told reporters, "All she ever said was that they were going out, just out. Sometimes she would stay until midnight, but usually we wanted her home by eleven."

On the last day they were seen alive, Elsie ate dinner at Mary's home, then the girls left on foot, purportedly en route to hang out with friends on Fort Lauderdale's Commercial Boulevard. Elsie had left a note for her half-brother, saying she expected to be home by 9:30 p.m., but that time came and went with no sign of either girl. In May 1973 the *Miami Herald* dubbed them runaways from home and high school, where both were new freshmen. Farmer's parents reported her missing on October 24, while the Briscolina's waited another week.

Neither family apparently gave any thought to foul play at the time. That would come later, in 1973, with discovery of both girls' skeletal remains.

But the Hangman knew already. He was keeping score.

*****

While the disappearances continued, Schaefer clung to his ludicrous fable regarding survivors Trotter and Wells. He'd meant them no harm, he told anyone who would listen, but had simply "overdone it" while trying to "teach them a lesson" about the perils of hitchhiking. His mother and sister believed him. Teresa Schaefer stood by her man at the time, though her dedication would waver, then collapse entirely, come spring of 1973.

Martin County prosecutors were less gullible. By Schaefer's own admission to the charges filed against him, he was guilty of both false imprisonment and aggravated assault, for holding Trotter and Wells tied up against their will. Only because both girls escaped without his aid was Schaefer spared two charges of attempted murder, for the nooses left around their necks. The ex-lawman, in his rational moments, knew he was bereft of a defense.

But he could still cut a deal.

With no lives lost or serious physical damage inflicted, the County offered Schaefer the bargain of a lifetime: plead guilty on one count of aggravated assault, while the other and both counts of false imprisonment were dismissed. Schaefer snapped up the deal and entered his plea in November 1972, before Judge D. C. Smith. In open court, Judge Smith called Schaefer "a perfect jackass and a thoughtless fool," but let the plea bargain stand. He sentenced Schaefer to one year in Martin County's jail, followed by three years' probation. If Schaefer kept his nose clean in the lockup, his year's incarceration would be cut in half for good behavior, freeing him in six short months.

And best of all, the execution of his sentence was deferred to January 15, 1973, giving him time to put his affairs in order. Come next June, he would be free to hunt again.

And in the meantime, he had two full months to kill.

*****

On January 7 or 8, 1973—accounts differ—19-year-old friends Collette Marie Goodenough and Barbara Ann Wilcox left Biloxi, Mississippi, where they had been visiting Collette's sister. The girls were last seen hitchhiking eastward, with plans to tour Florida. Eventually, their relatives assumed, both would return to their respective homes in Cedar Rapids, Iowa.

But they did not. The mystery surrounding them would only be resolved four years later, when skeletal remains of both young women surfaced at Port Saint Lucie in early 1977. At the time, no cause of death could be determined, but police already knew who'd buried them.

The Hangman had been busy as he waited for his turn in jail.

Chapter 5: Relics

Schaefer reported punctually to the Martin County jail on January 15, 1973. He loathed the idea of confinement but thought he had nothing to fear. Reduction of his charges meant potential freedom within half a year. Of course, he could behave himself in jail. Why not? By his own later estimate, the Hangman had been murdering since 1965, and he had slipped up only once. Granted, he couldn't be a cop again, even with forged letters of commendation, but so what? South Florida was full of jobs for able-bodied men. If nothing else, he could go back to guiding hunters in the Everglades. As for his lethal hobby, well, no one had turned up any of the bodies yet. He might go on indefinitely as he had before Trotter and Wells.

A hint that he was wrong surfaced two days after he entered jail, on January 17. That Wednesday afternoon, construction workers at a job site near Plantation High School unearthed Elsie Lina Farmer's skeletal remains. Nearly a month passed before Mary Alice Briscolina's bones were excavated from a grave 200 yards away from Farmer's final resting place. Dental records identified both missing girls, but nothing found at autopsy revealed their cause of death.

If Schaefer read or heard the news, he gave no sign of it. He had a new hobby inside: writing more gruesome stories of the kind he'd earlier abandoned and put in storage at his mother's home. After the fact, Emerson "Gene" Floyd, the Hangman's cellmate for six weeks, described Schaefer's long hours writing tales. "He wouldn't show it to us," Floyd told the *Miami Herald.* "He'd lay in his bunk and write and read his writing to us. I tell you, there were some hair-raising things. It was mostly just brutal. He said he was going to sell his writing in a book."

*****

It turned out that police who spoke with Lucille Place in September 1972 were not quite as lazy as she supposed. They *did* trace the license number she provided for Jerry Shepherd's car, unaware—as she was—that the number furnished lacked one vital digit. Aside from personalized or "vanity" plates, all tags issued began with numbers based on Florida's 67 counties ranked by population. Thus, Dade, Duval and Hillsborough Counties were numbered 1, 2 and 3, respectively, on down the list to Liberty County at 67 with less than 9,000 year-round inhabitants. In 1972, Pinellas County ranked fourth in line, presumably the source of Jerry Shepherd's license tag which Mrs. Place had copied down as 4D1728, omitting the second digit "2." The "D" meant it was issued to a compact car. Officers traced that license to a resident of St. Petersburg who bore no resemblance to Shepherd, owned an entirely different make of car, and had an iron-clad alibi for last September 27.

There matters rested until a Sunday in March 1973, when Ira and Lucille Place happened to drive through Stuart, two counties north of their home. Glancing around, Lucille noted that many automobile tags started with the number 42—Martin County's rank in population at that time. (Today it lists as number 31.) A revelation struck Lucille, as if the suspect murder car was there before her once again. "My God," she blurted out to Ira. "He's from this county!"

This time, Lucille ran down the license tag herself, finding a bluish-colored Datsun registered to Gerard Schaefer. In her mind, "Jerry Shepherd" was a simple—even simple-minded—alias. Calling unannounced at Schaefer's last address, an apartment complex, she spoke to the manager and learned that Schaefer was currently in jail for abducting and assaulting two young women. From that house call, Mrs. Place proceeded to the Martin County Sheriff's office, where she viewed a mug shot of Schaefer and quickly branded him the "Jerry Shepherd" who had driven off with Susan and friend Georgia in September.

Some time later, William Hutchins also viewed Schaefer's Datsun, pronouncing it the car that took his wife, Belinda, on her last known ride in January 1972, eight months before Susan Place and Georgia Jessup disappeared.

Those identifications of Schaefer's sedan were suggestive, but they proved nothing on which charges might be based. Driving someone away from home is not a crime. Without dead bodies, the *corpus delicti,* there was no proof of a single homicide, much less three. On March 25, Susan Place's parents visited the Martin County jail. Schaefer refused to speak with them, but jailers showed them Schaefer's mug shot and they made another positive I.D., Lucille Place saying, "There's no question in our minds." A deputy went back to Schaefer's cell, bearing a photograph of Susan, but the Hangman denied ever seeing her before. The deputy asked Schaefer if he'd take a polygraph exam. Schaefer refused.

"So where does that leave me?" Lucille asked journalists rhetorically. "It leaves me unglued."

Next, investigators checked out "Jerry Shepherd's" link to Colorado, and specifically the university he claimed to have attended there. No college in the Mile-High State had any records of a Jerry Shepherd or Gerard Schaefer enrolled in classes. A routine bulletin to Colorado law enforcement, seeking information on the whereabouts of Susan Place or Georgia Jessup, likewise scored no hits.

No solid evidence existed yet to contradict Schaefer's denials of involvement with the missing girls, but the Hangman was concerned. According to Gene Floyd, soon after pleading ignorance of them, Schaefer tore up his jailhouse writings and flushed their shredded pieces down the toilet in their cell.

*****

Schaefer's luck took a radical turn for the worse on April 1, 1973. That Sunday afternoon, three Martin County men went out to Hutchinson Island, bent on collecting aluminum cans for resale as scrap metal. They walked along Blind Creek, which bisects the island on an east-west axis in territory claimed by St. Lucie County. Instead of finding scrap, however, they discovered parts of a dismembered human body. Looking closer, they realized the grisly relics belonged to *two* victims, including both torsos, arms and legs, but no heads.

The body parts lay scattered around a square hole, some six feet long and two feet deep, partly concealed by ficus trees. It seemed to be a shallow grave unearthed by woodland scavengers, who had dispersed the pit's contents for several yards around while feeding on the victims' flesh.

But had those scavengers removed both heads?

St. Lucie County's sheriff's officers, led by Lieutenant Pat Duval, rushed to the scene. Duval described the sight for reporters, saying, "It was brutal and weird. They [the victims] were girls, and it looked as though they were cut up by a big strong man with a heavy machete or knife. Several of the bones were cut clear through."

Before disturbing any evidence, Duval summoned Dr. H. H. Schofield, Chief Medical Examiner for St. Lucie County. Viewing the truncated remains, Schofield opined that they'd been severed "with the precision of a butcher," pointing out deep knife marks on the exposed root of a tree near the open grave, suggesting the killer had used it as his "chopping block." Directly overhead, a stout limb bore apparent rope marks on its smooth bark. Farther down the trunk, someone had carved the initials "C. J.," later surmised to stand for Crystal Jessup. Officers sawed off the branch and knife-scarred root, while photographing the etched initials.

The victims' torsos proved both victims had been female. One was nude, the other partly covered with a pair of blue jeans bearing three embroidered patches. One depicted an owl, the second a crescent moon with a star at its center, and the third a cartoon roadrunner calling, "Beep Beep." Lieutenant Duval told gathering reporters, "We are hoping that those patches will eventually enable us to identify the girl who was wearing the jeans."

Physical remains included an arm with a narrow belt fastened around one wrist, suggesting that its owner was suspended from the nearby tree at some point during her ordeal. One torso lay at the lip of the opened grave, while the other was 50 feet away. From the pit itself, officers excavated a salmon-colored halter top, two pink full-length slips, a pink bikini top, and an empty wine bottle. One published report adds "a dozen pair of pantyhose" to the formerly buried cache. Another pile of clothing nearby included a medium-size tee shirt, a pink dress, a woman's black shoe with a two-inch spike heel, and a pair of white panties.

Sundown ended the search, but deputies remained on guard throughout the night over the roped-off crime scene. Bright and early next morning, the hunt resumed, discovering two human jawbones—one upper, one lower, both with teeth attached. Dr. Schofield examined both, suggesting that they came from different skulls. Dr. Richard Souviron of Coral Gables, a member of the American Board of Forensic Odontology and president of its ethics committee, examined both jaws and compared them with known dental records of the two missing girls. He had no difficulty matching Susan Place's jaw, and felt certain the other belonged to Georgia Jessup, pending further study. "I would say," he told reporters, "it's one in a thousand it's anyone else." Dr. Schofield's autopsy revealed that both girls had been dead between four and six months, Place suffering a gunshot to the jaw.

The island grave's location brought to mind two other cases from the same vicinity. Most recent was the chance discovery of a man's mutilated body on January 3, found planted in an 18-inch-deep grave, located a few hundred yards from Blind Creek. Officers had identified that victim as Leonard Masar, 45-year-old proprietor of a West Palm Beach coffee shop, found with his hands severed prior to burial, but they had no leads to his killer. Stretching farther back to July 1972, kidnap victims Nancy Trotter and Pamela Wells had escaped the Hangman's clutches roughly eight miles south of the new murder site.

Young women bound to trees and left to suffer, possibly to die. That case, detectives knew, had already been cleared. The man responsible was doing time in Martin County's jail. Ira and Lucille Place had identified that inmate as the man last seen with their daughter and Georgia Jessup. Now, all police needed was hard evidence to lock him up for good.

Driving that search for proof was Robert Stone, admitted to the Florida Bar in 1964, then assistant public defender and later City Prosecutor in Fort Pierce. In 1972, he won election as the first full-time State Attorney of the 19th Judicial Circuit, spanning Indian River, Martin, Okeechobee, and St. Lucie Counties, winning subsequent four-year terms without opposition. Stone soon set his sights on Schaefer and was not about to let him slip away.

*****

On April 7, 1973, police served a search warrant on the Fort Lauderdale home occupied by Doris and Teresa Schaefer, at 2716 Southwest 34th Avenue. Their son/husband had stashed some of his personal belongings there, in a locked spare bedroom no one was supposed to enter, and authorities were anxious to examine them.

Various media accounts summarize the searchers' findings at Doris Schaefer's home, often garbling, exaggerating, or understating the objects retrieved. The only reliable source is a six-page typewritten inventory obtained from the Broward County Sheriff's Department, listing 10 exhibits, most with multiple items logged separately into evidence. That stash included:

Exhibit 1: A paperback book titled *The History of Torture,* with Schaefer's name written inside the cover and an attached note reading "To John from Cindy"; a paper folder containing 17 strips of photo negatives depicting naked women; an envelope addressed to Schaefer from a New York publishing house, returning a letter from Schaefer that sought information on executions of women with a note reading, "Can't help you with the information you requested"; an envelope with the return address of Florida Atlantic University, containing 14 black-and-white photos "of the buttocks and crotch of a figure dressed in women's undergarments"; and a small vial containing two human teeth with gold fillings.

Exhibit 2: A Kodak film negative strip with four shots of "what appears to be a female buttocks and crotch area."

Exhibit 3: An empty box in which handcuffs are sold and three penknives, two with brown handles and one black.

Exhibit 4: A seven-page typescript with additional handwritten notes, detailing the torture and death by hanging of a woman in a swampy area; a five-page handwritten story portraying the murder of a woman dressed as a waitress, slain near Powerline Road, aka State Road 85 in Broward and Palm Beach Counties; six pages of handwriting about women urinating as they're hanged in Germany's Hamburg Railroad Station, attached to a manila envelope addressed to "Jerry Shepard" at Doris Schaefer's home; a three-page handwritten story of another German woman's hanging, including the name Michelle Dumont; a one-page handwritten account of prisoner Eleanor Hussy's hanging in London, in June 1760; one page with handwriting on both sides, discussing the proper method of executing a woman and mutilating her body; three typed pages presenting a killer's first-person story of hanging a woman named Carmen, dressed in a pink nightgown that reveals her blonde pubic hair, also naming another victim as Sonora Nia and describing a triple hanging of females; eight typed pages portraying vivid descriptions of the author killing a woman clad in a black chiffon dress and matching panties, with her hair done up, afterward dismembered with her teeth pulled and her body dumped in a canal; 11 handwritten pages that "keep jumping from story to story," including a description of the killer pulling gold teeth from a female victim's mouth; three typed pages on the hanging of an Irish "harlot," dated December 1970 and bearing the byline of "Jerry Sheperd"; one typed page portraying the murder and burial of a waitress, after her slayer removed all I.D.; three pages of handwritten notes on women hanged by Nazis and partisans during World War II; one handwritten page sketching the murder of another young white girl; three pages of handwritten notes of a young blonde's hanging, naming her executioner as "Jack"; and a three-page handwritten story set somewhere in Latin America, with revolutionaries whipping and hanging young women.

Exhibit 5: One manila envelope, otherwise undescribed; a magazine cover depicting a man and woman, with a noose drawn around the woman's neck; one black-and-white photo of a woman having sex with two men; a page torn from a magazine depicting a nude woman with handwritten notes plus a drawing of a bullet hole and blood; another magazine page showing a woman in black lingerie; two index cards bearing "poems about hanging women"; five index cards depicting attire worn by women on the gallows; a one-page handwritten story of a woman hanged while wearing a green skirt and "water proof underwear"; 21 typewritten pages recounting more hangings of women and "imaginary stories" of the New York City Police Department; five handwritten pages recounting more women's hangings, naming one victim as Mary Former; five pages of drawing in which women are hanged while their male executioners make various comments; one copy of *Today's Nudist* magazine with "various writings entered under pictures"; one issue of *Wow Nude* magazine with nooses drawn around the necks of certain models; and one "picture of [a] male and female together."

Exhibit 6: One copy of the *Fort Lauderdale News*, dated December 26, 1970; one page from the sports section of the *Fort Lauderdale News*, dated December 23, 1970; an unnamed Fort Lauderdale newspaper, dated September 27, 1970, with an article on page 11B headlined "Jury Probes Hanging Death"; and Section C from the *Fort Lauderdale News*, dated June 14, 1970, bearing an article on the disappearances of Leigh Bonadies and Carmen Hallock, titled "Two Women Lost in Mystery Web."

Exhibit 7: A small gold jewelry box containing: a bracelet with gold mesh braid; a silver charm bracelet with five heart-shaped charms inscribed "D.R.," "B," "M.T.N.," "Ruth," and "Papa"; a silver bracelet bearing rose-shaped beads, plus a cross and a Madonna medal at the clasp; a red leather bracelet "attached to a four leaf clover design"; a gold chain 17¾ inches long; a silver charm bracelet with one charm in the shape of Louisiana, stamped "New Orleans" and initials "C.P.A.I." plus the date 1960; a pair of women's earrings in a pink circular design; a woman's silver pin in the shape of a man, cast in green glass; a gold medal with initials "CX" above two swimmers and the words "Participant Exchange Meet"; a "Tri-Hi-Y" pin from the YMCA, with a red torch on a blue background; a green pin with a red cross in its upper corner, above the legend "Home Nursing"; a round pin with a silver cloverleaf design set on a blue background; a fish-shaped pin in blue, green and orange; a "very small" wooden cross; two small jackknives, one ¼ of an inch long, the other ½ inch; a pair of gold scissors about ¾ of an inch long; a reindeer pin about ½ inch long; two gold nutcrackers, each one inch long; and a small gold pin in the shape of a cheerleader's megaphone, bearing the word "Pep."

Exhibit 8: One canvas backpack; two red pens; a paperback book titled *Scorpio*; a box of Fire Chief matches; one silver "Indian bracelet with Indian designs"; one letter opener with a brass handle; one Curad adhesive bandage; one suede woman's purse containing miscellaneous coupons; a leather folder titled "Secret Path"; the birth certificate of Barbara Ann Wilcox, naming her parents and listing their address in Cedar Rapids; and five items belonging to Collette Marie Goodenough—her passport, Iowa driver's license, an Air Force dependent's I.D. card, another I.D. card from a "Special Problems Center," and a notebook filled with poems she had written, the last entry dated December 7, 1972.

Exhibit 9: A White Owl Ranger cigar box containing: an airmail envelope addressed to G. Schaefer, with a return address for John O'Reilly in Victoria, Australia; a handwritten letter to "Buddy," describing the murder and mutilation of women by "wogs" in the Sahara Desert portion of Morocco; 37 black-and-white photos of naked women being hanged and mutilated, with handwritten notations on the back of each; four airmail envelopes with no addresses, bearing canceled stamps from Helvetia, Switzerland; a plain envelope addressed to "Gerald J. Schaefer Jr." at his mother's house, postmarked from Australia, with 54 black-and-white photos of nude, mutilated women inside, six bearing handwritten notes on the back; another envelope from Australia, addressed to G. J. Schaefer at his mother's home, containing 13 black-and-white photos of naked women, one decapitated, 11 others being hanged; one Florida Power and Light envelope with a stamped return address for "Holfelner—Gonia Crouse PA" in Fort Lauderdale.

Exhibit 10: Two black cash drawers; a canvas bag bearing the label "Federal Reserve Bank, Jacksonville, Florida"; a blue zippered coin bag labeled "First National Bank of Fort Lauderdale"; a canvas bag labeled "First Security Corporation Banks Utah, Wyoming and Idaho"; and a brown bag labeled "Farmer's Bank & Savings Company, Pomeroy, Idaho."

That, according to police, is the sum total of evidence seized from Doris Schaefer's home on April 7. To that roster, the *Miami Herald* added a "collection of shotguns and handguns and knives," while *Inside Detective* magazine mentioned "lengths or rope, several rifles and hunting knives," the I.D. of a man named Ted Greer (never located), plus an unspecified number of bones police "speculated were wrist bones." *True Detective* described an "arsenal of knives" ranging from Japanese bayonets to butcher knives, machetes, and a switchblade. Yet another published account cites "11 guns and 13 knives," none mentioned anywhere in the sheriff's final inventory. But what they *did* find in Schaefer's secret stash was incriminating enough.

Aside from the Hangman's written descriptions of murder and mutilation, coupled with photos of apparent murder victims still unidentified today, officers retrieved physical items linking Schaefer to six missing and murdered women. He had I.D. for Collette Goodenough and Barbara Wilcox, along with Collette's book of poems. Newspaper clippings memorialized the disappearance of Leigh Bonadies and Carmen Hallock, for starters. Hallock's sister identified the four-leaf clover pin and several other pieces of jewelry as Carmen's. More tellingly, Hallock's dentist recognized the gold-filled teeth as hers. Gary Hainline also selected three pieces of jewelry as belonging to his vanished sister. Georgia Jessup's parents quickly identified the suede purse from Schaefer's stockpile. Another piece of jewelry had belonged to missing youngster Mary Briscolina, while an address book contained the name and address of grieving widower William Hutchins.

*****

Schaefer, of course, had a response for each piece of incriminating evidence collected from his mother's home. His gruesome stories were pure fiction, he insisted, and the mention of a "Carmen" in one story was coincidence. Doris Schaefer told reporters that the grisly prose sprang from Gerard's visits to the Henderson

Mental Health Center, during his time at Broward Community College, written on doctor's orders.

Perhaps.

Schaefer admitted knowing Leigh Bonadies, but said she'd left her jewelry with him as "collateral for a loan" she never repaid. As for Carmen Hallock's teeth, the Hangman had a suspect in her murder—and in that of Leigh Bonadies. The culprit, he claimed, was high school classmate and 1970 roomie Jack Dolan. During their time as roommates, Schaefer claimed, Dolan confessed to murdering Hallock *and* Leigh Bonadies. No doubt, he'd also placed Hallock's teeth where cops later found them, in a drawer of Schaefer's desk. Dolan, when questioned by Schaefer's defense attorney, angrily denied the charge, but remembered Schaefer telling him, "I like to kill...And he said he drank blood. He was laughing. He got a big joke out of it." Schaefer also collected skinning knives, carrying several in his car, along with guns, machetes and axes. Still unanswered is the question why, if Dolan had confessed two murders, future lawman Schaefer failed to share that information with authorities from 1970 until he faced a double murder charge three years later.

What of Collette Goodenough's passport, driver's license, two other I.D. cards, and book of handwritten poetry? The answer was simplicity itself. Schaefer had "found" the items at roadside during a routine patrol and, rather than deliver them to headquarters when Goodenough was listed as a missing person, chose instead to hide them at his mother's house. Why not, considering the other foolish things he'd done in uniform?

No one but Schaefer's family placed any stock in his attempts to brush aside the evidence in custody. Still, murder charges must be based on more than I.D. cards, pieces of jewelry, or even teeth—which may be lost in many ways without their owner landing somewhere in a shallow grave. Until bodies were found, and homicide determined as the cause of death, Schaefer would not be prosecuted for the deaths of Leigh Bonadies, Carmen Hallock, Belinda Hutchins, Collette Goodenough, or Mary Briscolina. On May 13, 1973, prosecutors charged him for the slayings of Susan Place and Georgia Jessup.

With any luck, that ought to take him off the streets for life.

Chapter 6: Media Monster

Schaefer's double murder charge, coupled with the evidence seized from his mother's home, created a sensation that spread swiftly from the Sunshine State, across America, and then around the world. State Attorney Robert Stone was first off the blocks, telling reporters, "I don't think the country has seen anything of this magnitude. It may be the greatest crime in the history of the United States." *Time* magazine claimed Schaefer was under investigation for "at least 20 murders," while the *Miami News* trumpeted: "Two murders linked to 26 Lost, Slain." On the day Schaefer was charged, the *Palm Beach Post-Times* raised the ante with a headline reading: "6 Dead; 28 May Be: A Trail of Butchered Girls."

Which girls?

Listed as "known dead, bodies found," the *Post-Times* named Susan Place and Georgia Jessup, Mary Briscolina and Elsie Farmer. Under "evidence of death, no body found," appeared the names of "Carman" Hallock and Leigh Bonadies. Cited as "missing, foul play suspected," the *Post-Times* mentioned four cases with eight victims total, discussed in more detail below. By actual count, then, the paper's list consisted of 14 presumed victims, less than half the number touted in its headline.

Who were the other missing girls? The *Post-Times* named Wendy Brown Stevenson and Peggy Rahn, whose case we already reviewed in Chapter 2. The only other persons named were sisters Katrina and Sandra Bivens, missing from Lake Park since January 1970. Finally came "two girls in Morgantown, W. Va." and "two girls in Grand Rapids, Iowa."

We may explain the last case first. There is no Grand Rapids in Iowa, though cities of that name exist in Michigan, Minnesota, Ohio and North Dakota. Clearly, the *Post-Times* garbled a reference to Collette Goodenough and Barbara Wilcox, who hailed from *Cedar* Rapids, Iowa, but disappeared in Florida and were not mentioned on the paper's list of missing women. If not for that clumsy *faux pas*, they would have been listed with Bonadies and Hallock under "evidence of death, no body found." Schaefer was never linked to any murders in the state of Iowa itself.

The Bivens sisters, reportedly aged 14 and 12, are more problematic. They allegedly vanished from Lake Park, in Palm Beach County, with coverage in the *Post-Times* furnishing no further details. Pursuing this elusive case long after the alleged double abduction, I found that no record of the sisters exists in the National Center for Missing and Exploited Children's database. I sent inquiries to the *Post* and Palm Beach County Sheriff's Department, but got no response from either. The Florida Department of Law Enforcement likewise had nothing on file, although they sent me an irrelevant 2005 report on the still-unsolved Leichner-Nater disappearances from 1966. Thankfully, I also contacted the Palm Beach County Library, where Government Research Services Librarian Jayme Bosio proved most helpful indeed. On September 16, 2016, she wrote to me:

> I searched the *Palm Beach Post* index and also found the May 1973 article regarding the missing Bivens sisters, which stated the girls had been missing since January 1970. I tried searching for articles on "Bivens" and limited it to January/February 1970 and found nothing. I tried "Bivens" and just 1970 and found nothing. I finally tried "missing girls" and "Lake Park" where the girls were from and found nothing. Using the term "missing girls" for the year 1970 retrieved numerous articles about Wendy Stevenson and Peggy Rahn, who went missing from Pompano Beach on December 29, 1969...Numerous articles about bringing in the FBI, clairvoyants, interviewing people

of interest, etc. But nothing about the Bivens sisters. It seems bizarre that two girls go missing after another set of girls go missing and it is not being reported.

Bizarre, indeed. What can it mean? How did reporters in 1973 find the names of two alleged missing girls that appear nowhere else in the public record? Unless further evidence appears, we have no proof the Bivens sisters ever lived, much less that they were murdered in Lake Park.

Finally, we have "two girls," apparently unknown, reported as still missing from West Virginia. That case deserves more explanation and reveals, as we shall see, that the *Post-Times* was wrong on both counts.

*****

Morgantown lies 1,084 miles north of the Hangman's normal hunting ground, but since Schaefer ultimately bragged of victims scattered "over three continents," no case that seems to fit his style is safely overlooked. On January 18, 1970, Karen Ferrell and Mared Malarik—both 19-year-old students at West Virginia University —left the Metropolitan Theater in downtown Morgantown after a screening of *Oliver*. Both veteran hitchhikers, they were last seen alive climbing into a cream-colored Chevrolet, driven by a man witnesses described as being in his forties. They never made it back to campus, and a $3,500 reward for leads to their whereabouts brought no takers until April 6, when state police received an anonymous letter signed with a triangle. It read:

Gentlemen,

I have some information on the whereabouts of the bodies of the two missing West Virginia University coeds, Mared Malarik and Karen Ferrell.

Follow directions very carefully—to the nth degree and you cannot fail to find them.

Proceed 25 miles directly South, from the Southern line of Morgantown. This will bring you to a wooded forest land. Enter into the forest exactly one mile. There are the bodies.

$25 + 1 = 26$ miles total.

Will reveal myself when the bodies are located.

Sincerely,

Δ

Governor Arch Moore Jr. directed officers to follow the letter's directions. On April 14 searchers found the two girls' headless bodies underneath a rough cairn of tree limbs and stones carried from a nearby creek, located six miles south of Morgantown. Their heads were missing, and an autopsy failed to reveal any lethal wounds beyond decapitation. A subsequent letter from "Δ" offered precise directions to the buried heads, but a second search revealed nothing. The heads remain missing today.

Seeking the killer, police turned to handwriting analysts, tracing the letters to one of three congregants from the 30-member Psychic Science Church in Cumberland, Maryland. One member, Fred Schanning, had consulted on the case with the church's leader, Rev. Richard Warren. Warren, in turn, sought help from the disembodied spirit of a 19th-century British physician he called "Dr. Spencer." Tape recordings of Warren's séances, channeling "Spencer," prompted them to write the letters received by police, with a third collaborator. In time, all three were cleared of involvement in the double murder.

An early suspect in the case, William Hacker, was arrested in Baltimore after he beheaded male victim Herbert Corbin on Christmas Eve 1970, but police found no link to the earlier crimes and left him to serve his life sentence in peace. Another West Virginia lifer, Edward Lee Fielder, confessed the double murder from prison, then clammed up and refused to say more, leaving detectives with nothing. Some amateur investigators blame serial killer Theodore Bundy for the slayings, while another accuses the rock group Ezra, because two girls were allegedly slain after one of its gigs in New Jersey. Other dark horse suspects include the unidentified "Mad Butcher," who dismembered victim Mike Rogers on Gauley Mountain in 1962, later killing at least seven more—and Mared Malarik's dentist, accused of molesting one female patient. He makes the list because Malarik had an appointment scheduled for the day after she disappeared, and because he called authorities to say Malarik might be seeking dental care. Sedatives he'd prescribed for her surfaced with her other belongings, near Grafton.

And then, of course, there's Gerard Schaefer Jr.

Suspected more because the coeds were beheaded, rather than for any other compelling reason, Schaefer was starting his third year in prison when police in West Virginia announced their solution to the Ferrell-Malarik case, in January 1976. Eugene Paul Clawson had been jailed since 1974 in Camden, New Jersey, for raping a 13-year-old girl and forcing a 15-year-boy into sex acts at gunpoint. Clawson's 73-page confession said he had kidnapped Ferrell and Malarik under threat of death and drove them to a secluded spot, where he handcuffed one and raped the other in his car, then switched them out to repeat the assault, before ordering them to have sex with each other. Afterward, he shot each in the head, severed their skulls with his brother's machete, then took the heads to show his sibling but the brother wasn't home. Frustrated, Clawson said he then buried the headless bodies and tossed both skulls into a ravine near his childhood home in Point Marion, Pennsylvania. Searchers there found no heads, but collected an old pair of handcuffs and some hair unearthed from an animal's den.

Clawson recanted his confession in May 1976, blaming a New Jersey cellmate for helping him make up the details. Why? In his delirium, Clawson believed that his acquittal in the West Virginia case would somehow nullify his sentence in New Jersey. Instead, Morgantown jurors convicted him in October and sentenced him to life. West Virginia's Supreme Court overturned that conviction in 1981 and ordered a new trial, where Clawson was acquitted, based on new medical evidence and a high-ranking policeman who voiced his conviction that Clawson's confession was false. Cleared on those counts, he returned to serve life in the Garden State, while the officer who'd supported him— Sergeant Robert Mozingo, now deceased—told reporters vaguely that he thought the killer was a classmate of the victims, never publicly identified.

But could the Hangman *possibly* have been responsible? We must say "yes," to the extent that nearly anything is "possible" in certain circumstances, but no evidence of any kind connects him to the West Virginia crimes, nor—unlike other murders he denied in public but confessed in private—did the case surface in any of his writings afterward.

For now, we set the unsolved case aside.

*****

Florida is known for executing murderers, but Schaefer would not face the death penalty for killing Susan Place and Georgia Jessup. On June 29, 1972, three months before the two girls vanished, the U.S. Supreme Court's five-to-four ruling in *Furman v. Georgia* invalidated capital punishment nationwide as "cruel and unusual punishment." The decision left states free to write new statutes, permitting executions for murder with various "special circumstances." In 1976 the Supreme Court overturned its *Furman* ruling and upheld the death penalty's constitutionality in the case of *Gregg v. Georgia*, but three more years elapsed before Florida resumed executions in 1979. Schaefer's only proven crimes occurred in legal no-man's land, meaning the worst that he could face was life imprisonment.

Public defender Elton Schwartz professed that even life inside might be too much, telling reporters and Judge Cyrus Pfeiffer Trowbridge that Schaefer suffered from a serious mental disorder. An expression of his client's innocence was tacked on almost as an afterthought. Judge Trowbridge sent Schaefer to the Florida State Hospital in Chattahoochee, built as an arsenal in the 1830s, converted to a prison in 1868, then refurbished to serve as a lunatic asylum in 1876. There, doctors would decide if the Hangman was legally sane and, therefore, fit for trial.

First in line, on April 10, was Dr. R. C. Eaton, who detailed Schaefer's background and noted that "from an early age he has had numerous sexual hangups." Schaefer also had "a considerable preoccupation with death, and would get excited when he dreamed about killing people. Sometimes he did not know what was fact and what was fantasy." Although "well oriented" during their interview, Schaefer "cried considerably, stating he felt there was no use in going on." He voiced suicidal thoughts in "a very matter-of-fact tone," saying he "definitely plans to go ahead with killing himself." Dr. Eaton found Schaefer "definitely depressed, partly as a reaction to the present situation," and recommended further evaluation.

Next up, on April 18, was Dr. Mordecai Haber, who reviewed Schaefer's troubled history, recording his lie that he failed at teaching "because they only wanted black people." Regarding his assault on victims Trotter and

Wells, Schaefer said, "I was mad at them. They laughed at me." He surprised Haber by confessing to acts of sodomy with cows and horses, sometimes after he'd beheaded them with a machete. Schaefer's future outlook was grim. "I'm going to kill myself," he said. "All this stuff about the murders. People are saying they've seen me with these girls and that I'm the last person to be seen with them. They say they have eyewitnesses. I don't know what to think." But Dr. Haber did, reporting that Schaefer "shows no symptoms or signs of organic brain damage, mental defect, or psychosis." His diagnosis was "antisocial personality, manifest by sexual deviation [and] erotic sadism." Haber deemed Schaefer mentally competent for trial.

Dr. Benjamin Ogburn interviewed Schaefer on June 20, finding the Hangman "well aware of his present situation and his reasons for admission to the hospital," although, oddly, "he denied any knowledge of the charges for which he is being held." Again, Schaefer admitted "suicidal reminations [sic]," fearing that "there might not be any way out, or any hope for him." When discussing his attacks on animals and other sadistic activity, "he would seem to smile inappropriately." Dr. Ogburn also spoke with wife Teresa, calling her "a somewhat niave [sic]" young woman who "denies any indication of psychiatric illness in her husband and has many doubts about the charges." Finally diagnosing

Gerard as a paranoid schizophrenic, Ogburn recommended "long-term in-patient psychiatric treatment. He is considered to be a very dangerous person, both to himself and to others."

Finally, on June 29, Schaefer met Dr. Hector Gianni. After recapping the subject's background, Gianni agreed with Dr. Ogburn, noting: "In general his affect appears appropriate, but sometimes he has an inappropriate smile in describing criminal fantasies that he wrote about or when he was referring to killing those people." Schaefer was "slightly depressed," but showed "a lot of preoccupation with his sexual experiences and fantasies." While judging that Schaefer's "recent memory was good," Gianni wrote that "his remote memory was poor about many different things." Concerning the Place-Jessup murders, "The patient also expressed to me several times that he is more worried about finding out whether or not he killed these girls than if he is found guilty or not of the crime." Gianni told Judge Trowbridge that Schaefer's confusion of fantasy and reality "creates doubts in my opinion if he will be able to aid his lawyer in his own defense."

Judge Trowbridge, for his part, had no such doubts. He scheduled Schaefer's trial for September 1973 on two counts of first-degree murder.

*****

When trial began on September 17, the prosecution's case consisted chiefly of eyewitness testimony and Schaefer's own words, committed to writing either as florid fiction or, as his mother insisted, part of some vague psychiatric prescription to cure his "hang-ups." Science identified the murdered girls but could not place Schaefer in their company. For that, the state relied on Ira and Lucille Place to identify Schaefer as the "Jerry Shepherd" who absconded with the victims one year earlier. Nothing but the suede purse retrieved from Doris Schaefer's home —identified as Georgia Jessup's by her parents— forged the final link to murder. Schaefer, for his part, insisted that he'd bought the purse in 1970 while visiting Morocco in the wake of his divorce. None of the evidence pointing a finger Schaefer's way for other homicides would be admissible in court.

On balance, Schaefer's written stories— published later, in the guise of "killer fiction"— seemed to weigh most heavily against him with the jurors chosen to decide his fate. One piece began: "In order to remain unapprehended, the perpetrator of an execution style murder such as I have planned must take precautions." Those included preparation of a grave beforehand, and construction of a makeshift gallows from sawhorses. He recommended beer "to induce urination and make the victim groggy and more cooperative," while soap "provides an excellent lubrication for anal intercourse." Nylon stockings should be used to bind a victim's hands and feet, and he suggested a douche bag for "a soapsuds enema which would be a great indignity, especially if one victim was made to urinate or defecate on the other."

A second story, told again in first-person narrative from the killer's point of view, described hanging a woman from a tree limb. After the murder, her killer goes home to eat dinner and sleep, then returns the next morning. "I will find the body hanging from the tree," he wrote, "and only then will I really notice it. Maybe fondle it and maybe even have coitus with it...I leave and then return so it will be unbelievable to myself that I did the deed. I will not be able to remember doing it. Funny isn't it[?]"

Jurors disagreed. They found nothing amusing in the Hangman's prose, nor were they fooled by his attempt to blame roommate Jack Dolan—long since cleared by homicide investigators—for "planting" the relics of dead women in Schaefer's cache of belongings. With that dodge deflated, Schaefer's defense veered to another track, asserting without any proof that crooked cops and mobsters had conspired to frame him in retaliation for his one-man crusade to purge Martin County of drug-related corruption. On September 27—one year to the day since Place and Jessup disappeared—the jury convicted Schaefer on both counts of murder.

97

Judge Trowbridge imposed the maximum sentence, two concurrent life terms, on October 4.

Chapter 7: Pen Pals

Inmate No. 035906 began his journey through Florida's penal system as do all male convicts, at Lake Butler's Reception and Medical Center, established in 1968 with twin missions of processing new inmates into the system and providing medical care to prisoners from all corners of the state. Aside from the standard examinations and orientation, Schaefer's future publicist would write that Lake Butler's guards "tortured" the Hangman, urging him to run so they could gun him down as an escapee. That alleged ordeal reportedly sent him to the lockup's hospital for six weeks.

It must have been there, then, that Teresa Schaefer paid her one and only prison visit to Gerard on November 17, 1973, announcing plans to divorce him and wed Elton Schwartz. She had "clicked" with Schwartz sometime during Schaefer's trial, though the attorney swore there was "no romance" involved before Schaefer's conviction. According to the *New York Times* and other sources, Schaefer gave his blessing to the happy couple and retained Schwartz as his counsel for the first of numerous appeals. Teresa received her uncontested divorce on November 21, newspapers announced Schwarz's proposal six days later, and the happy couple married on December 29.

By then, Schaefer had been transferred to Florida State Prison at Starke, where his publicist says he spent four years in solitary confinement with "no exercise, no sunshine, no fresh air, no law books." No record of his purported offense(s) has surfaced to date. During that period of isolation, Elton Schwartz took Schaefer's case to the Fourth District Court of Appeals, arguing that his client should have been indicted, rather than charged via "information," and should have faced a 12-member jury, rather than the six-member panel that convicted him. Florida Attorney General Robert Shevin, speaking for the state, claimed prosecutors gave Schaefer "the benefit of the doubt," trying him during a period when capital punishment was banned. His argument was meaningless, since charges are based on the date of the *crime,* not the *trial,* but Shevin won all the same, and Schaefer's appeal was denied. The Hangman forged ahead, filing 18 or 19 more appeals (reports differ) by 1987, when a weary judge barred him from lodging any more. "There has to be an end," that jurist said, "and a conclusion to litigation and to the abuse of the judicial process. The defendant should realize, once and for all, the die is cast, the mold is made, the loaf is baked."

Schaefer would find new ways to use the law for personal revenge in years to come.

Meanwhile, he kept an eye on news headlines and slowly, slowly worked to build a case that he had been the victim of a frame-up by his fellow Martin County deputies.

*****

On January 5, 1977, two men planning a barbecue on Leafy Road, found skeletal remains of two dismembered bodies in a thicket near the site of St. Lucie's present-day Oak Hammock Park. Sheriff's deputies recovered knotted rope or telephone wire (published reports vary), and a wooden crate they presumed was part of a crude gallows set-up. Dr. H. L. Schofield identified the bones as those of Barbara Wilcox and Collette Goodenough, reviving memories of Collette's possessions found at Doris Schaefer's home in April 1973. Questioned by the press, State Attorney Stone said, "It's not a matter of whether he did it or not. It's a matter of tying up a bunch of loose ends. You can't go to a grand jury with just a contention."

And once again, no charges would be filed.

November 1977 saw Schaefer released from solitary at Starke, allegedly with his "health in ruins" and "partially blind." Be that as it may, he was assigned to the prison law library, initially doing research for Sonia "Sunny" Jacobs, girlfriend of convicted cop killer Jesse Tafero.

Both were sentenced to die, with Jacobs landing at Starke since Florida had no death row for women at the time. Their case was controversial, and a male accomplice—Walter Rhodes—later confessed to killing both officers following Tafero's execution in May 1990. An appellate court overturned Sonia's death sentence in 1981, commuting it to life with a 25-year minimum. Schaefer turned Tafero's death into a graphic short story—titled "Jesse in Flames" because the prison's electric chair malfunctioned, setting Tafero's head on fire—and went on from there to become a jailhouse lawyer of some repute.

While he worked that first case, in April 1978, construction workers clearing fill dredged from a canal flanking the Amberwood development in Boca Del Mar, three miles southwest of Boca Raton, unearthed a human skull. Pathologists identified the victim as a woman, citing cause of death as "more than one bullet hole" in the skull. By mid-May the skull had been identified as that of Leigh Hainline Bonadies, some of whose belongings—the alleged collateral for an undocumented loan—had been found at Doris Schaefer's home five years earlier. No other trace of the body was found, and while reporters duly noted that "police have long investigated possible links between Schaefer and the disappearance of the Bonadies woman," no charges were filed. The case remains officially unsolved today.

On August 6, 1979, authorities transferred Schaefer from Starke to Avon Park Correctional Institution in Polk County, established in 1957 to confine minimum and medium custody male inmates. Two years before his move, it began accepting "close" custody convicts, but conditions were significantly better than at Starke. So much better, in fact, that Robert Stone told the *Stuart News,* in 1981, "That's too nice a place for him to be in. He ought to be in the worst possible prison in Florida." The same article mentioned two suspected victims from Wilton Manors: Bonnie Taylor, reported missing from the town "when Schaefer was operating a radar unit" for the local police department, and Cocoa Beach resident Patricia Wilson, vanished after an auto accident "police said Schaefer worked as a policeman." While the article's headline spoke of "charges waiting in the wings" for Schaefer, neither woman has been found to date, and he was never charged in either case. My several inquiries to Wilton Manors produced no further information.

*****

Four years after Stone's pronouncement, and one decade into Schaefer's imprisonment, he launched a plan to clear his name regarding crimes as yet unsolved. He used the mails to challenge various authorities, seeking to learn if they had any open cases pending on him in their several jurisdictions. Reporter Kameel Stanley would later write, in the *Tampa Bay Times,* that Schaefer "sent a letter to every sheriff in the state, asking them to check their records to see if he was a suspect in any open cases." If true, those letters have been lost, but Schaefer himself preserved copies of seven missives received from various authorities he contacted between December 1982 and May 1983. All entered the public domain as exhibits in the 1993 federal case of *Schaefer v. Newton and Avon Books.*

The first letter in Schaefer's file, dated December 23, came from Captain Kelton Wheeler of the Pompano Beach Police Department's Investigative Division, confirming that Schaefer had volunteered for a polygraph test to clear him of suspicion in the disappearances of Peggy Rahn and Wendy Stevenson. "After a careful analysis," Captain Wheeler wrote, he found "no deceptive criteria" in Schaefer's denials of abducting and killing the girls, or of "knowing for sure" what happened to them. In closing, Kelton wrote: "I want to personally thank you for volunteering for this examination and to state that you are no longer considered a suspect in the disappearance of Peggy Rahn and Wendy Stephenson [*sic*]."

Thomas Newbraugh, prosecuting attorney for Monongahela County, West Virginia, wrote to the Hangman next, on December 28, informing Schaefer of Eugene Clawson's conviction in the case of Karen Ferrell and Mared Malarik. Schaefer sought no revised opinion from Newburgh after the Clawson case fell through, assuming that he ever heard the news.

The next letter to Schaefer, dated January 12, 1983, came from State Attorney Janet Reno in Miami, still nine years away from her appointment as U.S. Attorney General. Crisp and to the point, it said: "Based on the limited information you provided us, we find no record of pending charges against you. Our office would have information only if charges had been filed." Since Schaefer had not been accused of claiming any victims in Miami, call that one a wash.

On January 25, Schaefer got his answer from the 18th Judicial Circuit. Penned by Phillip Sellers, chief investigator for State Attorney Douglas Chesney Jr., the letter affirmed that there were "no indictments, warrants, capias, summons, or other documents requiring your presence in either Brevard or Seminole County." It was another pointless inquiry, since none of Schaefer's alleged crimes occurred in either jurisdiction.

Writing one day later, January 26, Chief Assistant State Attorney Ralph Ray Jr. responded to three Schaefer letters, saying, "This office has no homicide cases being actively investigated wherein you are considered a suspect." That covered Broward County, where the Hangman definitely *was* suspected of multiple murders, though insufficient evidence existed to indict or try him.

Next, on April 25, Acting Major B. Pitts, chief of detectives for the Avon Park Police Department, mailed another pointless denial that Schaefer was suspected "in any homicide case currently under investigation by this Department." No one had linked his name to any, but the Hangman made a show of covering all bases.

Finally, on May 31, Deputy Chief Investigator John Dale wrote from the 20th Judicial District, covering Charlotte, Collier, Glades, Hendry and Lee Counties. "As of this date," the letter read, "all law enforcement agencies in our Circuit which might have had any interest in you have been heard from with negative results. In view of the above, we are closing your file in our office." What file? To this day, no published source has linked Schaefer to any deaths or disappearances in the 20th District.

Wasted time and postage, but time was one thing Schaefer had to spare. Years later, his publicist would release those letters in a packet labeled "Gerard John Schaefer Cleared of Crimes," as if they had proved anything at all.

Meanwhile, the Hangman occupied himself with other things.

*****

In 1979 Schaefer announced his marriage to "Elen," a young Filipina mail-order bride who'd corresponded with him from her rural village, sending a photograph inscribed "To my loving husband Gerard." Elen finally reached the States in July 1980, settling for the moment in St. Petersburg with Schaefer's father and Gerard Sr.'s second wife. A marriage license materialized as if by magic, persuading officials at Avon Park to grant the happy couple contact visits. Over the next five years, Elen drifted back and forth between the homes of Schaefer's parents, then received her long-awaited green card and dropped her lifer husband like the proverbial hot potato.

In January 1985, Elton Schwartz ceased representing Schaefer in his various appeals. The Hangman barely seemed to notice, busy as he was with other things. Marriage aside, he adopted a series of female personas—dominatrix "Mistress Felice," prostitute "Jessica Zurriaga," grim "Matron Miller," a husband-killer awaiting execution—and so forth. Enticing correspondence brought cash dribbling in, with a bonus from "submissives" who paid for the privilege of laundering Mistress Felice's used panties (soiled and mailed by "a lady" outside prison). Within three years, Schaefer claimed to run a "slave empire" of some 500 correspondents who'd answered his ads in various sex magazines. The list included cons in other prisons, who would ultimately learn of Schaefer's ruse and spread the word through cellblock channels to his detriment.

A variation of that theme in 1984 cast Schaefer in the role of 14-year-old hooker "Dee Dee Kelly," collaborating with U.S. Postal Inspectors and police in North Miami to build a case against British-born Mervyn Harold "Eric" Cross, a "child porn king" operating internationally despite his confinement in Florida. While Schaefer—as "Dee Dee"—offered photographs for sale to pedophiles, Cross paid Gerald Sr. a monthly stipend for use of his phone line to contact colleagues in the Philippines. Feds listened in and collected answers from "Dee Dee's" customers, ultimately filing new charges on Cross and extending his sentence, while both Schaefer's and "Dee Dee's" sundry correspondents escaped prosecution.

Meanwhile, as a self-taught jailhouse lawyer, Schaefer wrote briefs for fellow cons to help with their appeals. It boosted Schaefer's popularity at first, before he started poaching customers from other locked-down "legal eagles," but as usual, he put his own peculiar, self-destructive twist on the equation. While debriefing inmate clients, Schaefer milked them for the details of their cases, then betrayed them if it worked to his advantage with authorities. One inmate, never publicly identified, was pending trial for murder when he told "attorney" Schaefer where to find the victim's corpse. Faster than you can say "sell-out," Schaefer informed police, who used the evidence to place his client on death row.

It was another strike against the Hangman as a jailhouse snitch.

*****

Before his third marriage evaporated, Schaefer sat with psychologist Frances Miller at Avon Park on March 20, 1985. Miller described her report as "a psychological evaluation...[that] provides a current mental state as well as psychological test data." Specifically, the Minnesota Multiphasic Personality Inventory, America's most widely used and researched standardized psychometric test of adult personality and psychopathology, showed "marked improvement in this man's personality growth and...has shown no pathology." Schaefer had sought bi-weekly counseling for the past year "to better understand himself and to gain tools for coping with prison life." His father's recent death had "tested" Schaefer, but Miller wrote that the Hangman "appears to be stable, more in control of himself and more potentially capable of conducting a responsible life at this time." Above all, Schaefer did not "appear manipulative to this therapist," revealing no "overt mental disorder, nor was there any suggestion of a potential for such a problem in the future."

Imagine Miller's surprise, five months later, when Schaefer was charged with plotting to escape from Avon Park and kill a list of enemies including ex-wife Teresa, ex-defender Elton Schwartz, State Attorney Robert Stone, and Judge C. Pfeiffer Trowbridge. His reward for that scheme, on August 21, was a transfer back to maximum security at Starke, in Bradford County. Six days later, Elton and Teresa Schwartz acquired pistol permits. In October, Robert Stone resigned as state attorney, four months into his latest four-year term. Schaefer claimed Stone was afraid of his "corruption" being bared. Stone cited "personal reasons" for retiring.

*****

Aside from long-distance scams and squealing on his fellow convicts, Schaefer derived satisfaction from fraternizing with other deviant killers at Starke. One who figured in the Hangman's correspondence was Bernard Eugene Giles, a necrophiliac serial killer born in April 1953, serving life for murdering five Brevard County teenagers between September and November 1973, plus another 15 years for lesser charges and a final 15 years for escape in September 1981. Schaefer liked talking to Giles—and writing about him to "free world" correspondents— because Giles first killed his victims, then left them exposed to Florida's sun until they "got

110

ripe," at which time he would "climb aboard" for sex.

On balance, after reading Schaefer's private letters and his published "fiction," the pair had much in common.

Another Starke inmate who amused Schaefer was Gerald Eugene Stano, a rape-slayer of female prostitutes, hitchhikers and runaways ranging from Florida northward to Pennsylvania and New Jersey. New York born as Paul Zeininger in September 1951, Stano suffered such neglect from his unmarried mother that when she finally placed him up for adoption, six months later, doctors found him functioning at "an animalistic level," even eating his own feces to survive. Finally adopted by a nurse and her husband, who gave him their last name, Stano wet his bed until the age of 10 and proved a lackluster student in school, aside from excelling at music. In high school, where he lingered until age 21 before finally achieving "social promotion," Stano once stole money from his father, bribing other members of the track team to let him win a race and thereby break his record for consistent failure. Stano claimed his first victim at age 18, totaling 41 by the time of his arrest in April 1980. Some investigators doubted his marathon confessions, but it hardly mattered. Convicted of nine homicides, Stano earned a death sentence and kept his date with "Old

Sparky"—the state's electric chair—in March 1998.

After they met at Starke, Schaefer enjoyed teasing Stano with comparative body counts. As Schaefer wrote, "He said he got more kills than Ted Bundy. I told him I had more than him and Ted put together. He could only blink his eyes and make a little 'o' mouth like a whistle pucker. It hurt him."

*****

And speaking of Theodore Robert Bundy, he was the star of Schaefer's limited universe, dubbed "The Society of Fiends" when the Hangman set pen to paper. Born Theodore Robert Cowell, out of wedlock in November 1946, Bundy was 23 before he learned that his "elder sister" was in fact his mother. Arrested twice in high school, on suspicion of burglary and auto theft, he dropped out of college in his junior year, then dabbled in politics before devoting himself to murdering young women between 1974 and 1978. The trail of bodies spanned America, from the Pacific Northwest into Utah and Colorado, finally ending in Florida with his chance arrest by an officer on routine patrol. Bundy decapitated at least 12 of his victims, keeping some of their heads in his apartment as trophies, cremating one in a girlfriend's fireplace, and he sometimes revisited his body dump sites over long periods of time, grooming and copulating with the corpses until decomposition and the ravages of wild scavengers made further interaction unfeasible. Convicted of three Florida murders in 1980, he received death sentences in two separate trials and landed in Starke, where the Hangman awaited him.

When they met in 1986, Schaefer would write, "I recognized at once the famous smirking face, and my heart skipped a beat as Ted Bundy fixed his gaze on me with a sudden grin of recognition as if he were meeting an old friend." By Schaefer's account, Bundy wasted little time in voicing hero-worship, claiming he recognized Schaefer from photos published in detective magazines during 1973, months before Bundy's first confirmed murder. Better yet, from Schaefer's viewpoint, Bundy claimed he had patterned his first double murder—of Washington victims Denise Naslund and Susan Ott in July 1974—on the Hangman's reported penchant for "playing doubles." Needless to say, Schaefer had to lord it over Bundy, later writing:

> Ted was, of course, a tyro when he nabbed Ott and Naslund; when I nabbed Jessup and Place I had been in the ghoul game for almost 10 years...By then I was into doing double murders and an occasional triple when the opportunity

arose...Ted was playing at copycat and doing a poor job of it at that.

Which didn't stop the two psychopaths from becoming friends—or, as Schaefer might have said, master and acolyte. Along the way, Schaefer gloated, "I stoked his sense of depravity and encouraged him to reveal his true nature," reaching a point where Bundy shrugged off Schaefer's superior body count, insisting that "he was the Best because he had a much more developed sense of depravity."

And Schaefer did more. As Bundy's appeals fizzled out, advancing the date of his own death, the Hangman encouraged him to extend his life by confessing—in effect, trading the sites of hidden corpses for successive stays of execution. On the side, they discussed "the maggot problem" and techniques for cleaning seat covers when victims urinated in their cars. Before Bundy took his final walk to Old Sparky, he had confessed 30 murders in seven states, while sometimes hinting that the true number might run to triple digits. Various law enforcement agencies believe his final count was too conservative, some officers suggesting that his killing spree began in 1969—and perhaps as early as 1961, when Ted was only 15.

*****

In January 1988, another Schaefer enemy, Judge Pfeiffer Trowbridge, resigned from the bench in Martin County. The Hangman, in typical style, blamed his departure on fear of some revelation in the offing, but Schaefer had no aces up his sleeve.

At Starke, Schaefer received another 30 days in solitary, as he put it, "for submitting a story to a magazine. The editor was so upset he wrote to the prison demanding I be punished." The offending article, according to its author, was "a biker's testimonial" submitted to an unnamed magazine of the sort that cater to "outlaw" motorcycle enthusiasts. Or, as Schaefer saw it, "Red hot smoking gospel from the mouth of a Scooter Tramp turned to Jesus," as told to the Hangman in prison. Perhaps it was the "murder, sex perversion...[and] maggots up the nose" that prompted the anonymous editor's reaction— assuming Schaefer's punishment had anything at all to do with writing.

Whatever the truth, he left solitary on October 20, 1988, and was shuttled off to Marion Correctional Institution in Ocala, opened in 1959 as a women's prison, but equipped since 1976 with a separate block for male inmates. The transfer, whatever its motivation, proved to be short lived. By November 3, the Hangman was back at Starke. The Florida Department of Corrections scheduled Schaefer's first parole hearing for 2017. He would be 71 years old, assuming he survived that long inside.

Chapter 8: Ottis and Adam

While Schaefer reveled in Ted Bundy's adulation, he preferred the company of Ottis Elwood Toole, a self-proclaimed serial killer of global renown whose on-and-off confessions linked him to more than 100 murders committed with friend and occasional gay lover Henry Lee Lucas. Florida juries convicted Toole of two murders in 1984, imposing death sentences for both, later reduced on appeal to life imprisonment. In 1991 he admitted four more killings, receiving quadruple life terms. That total hardly qualified as something special in the Sunshine State, but Toole had other qualities that recommended him to Schaefer as a pen pal.

Born in Jacksonville, one year to the month after Schaefer, Toole boasted a family beside which Schaefer's "conflictual" brood paled by comparison. Toole's father was a drunk who left their home to live with his own sister as man and wife, offering Ottis to male friends as a sex toy from age five onward. Between molestations, Toole's sisters dressed him as a girl, unconsciously encouraging the homosexuality that came to dominate his life around age 10. Toole's mother was a fanatical Christian fundamentalist, her Bible-thumping offset by the boy's maternal grandmother—a self-styled satanic witch who took him on grave-robbing expeditions to obtain components for various magical potions. Grandma dubbed Ottis "the devil's child." His first murder, Toole always claimed, had been a salesman who picked him up for sex at age 14. After his crimes went public in 1983, locals called him "The Jacksonville Cannibal."

Toole was, to say the least, no match for Schaefer when it came to wits. Barely literate, an epileptic who also suffered from dyslexia and attention deficit hyperactivity disorder, Toole had made matters worse with decades of heavy drinking and habitual drug abuse. A lifelong fire-setter, he was serving time at Raiford for torching abandoned homes in Jacksonville before epic confessions added murder charges to his rap sheet, saying of the houses he had burned, "I just hated to see them standing there." In prison, he swilled bootleg hooch and popped whatever pills might be available, while servicing a list of cons who called him "Grandma." Police and prosecutors nationwide debated the veracity of Toole's confessions, often paired with those of Lucas from his Texas cell, but one stood out above the rest.

Around noon on July 21, 1981, Revé Walsh took six-year-old son Adam shopping with her at the Hollywood Mall, at Hollywood Boulevard and North Park Road in Hollywood, Florida. In the mall's Sears store, she left Adam with other boys at a kiosk of video games, to visit the nearby lamp department, and returned at 12:15 to find the kiosk abandoned. The store's manager told Mrs. Walsh a scuffle had erupted among the boys, whereupon a security guard ordered all of them to leave the store. When a 90-minute search failed to locate Adam, accompanied by announcements broadcast over the mall's public address system, Mrs. Walsh summoned police at 1:55. Their canvass proved fruitless. Adam had simply vanished.

Twenty days later, on August 10, two fishermen hauled a boy's severed head from a drainage canal beside the Florida Turnpike at Vero Beach, 130 miles north of Hollywood. Divers plumbed the murky waters without finding any more remains. Police announced that dental records—more specifically, a single filling in a molar—matched Adam's, but that finding has since been challenged. A coroner pegged suffocation as the cause of death, with decapitation occurring postmortem. According to his report, death had occurred several days before discovery of the head. Revé Walsh and husband John couldn't bear to view what remained of their child, sending a family friend instead to complete visual identification. No other trace of Adam Walsh has been recovered to this day.

The tragedy placed John Walsh in the spotlight as a newly minted crusader for justice and victim rights advocate, particularly in regard to children. Soon after Adam's disappearance,

119

John and his wife founded the Adam Walsh Child Resource Center, a non-profit organization dedicated to legislative reform, soon merged with the National Center for Missing and Exploited Children, which welcomed John onto its board of directors. On October 10, 1983, NBC television aired *Adam,* a dramatization of the still-unsolved crime, with Daniel Travanti cast as John Walsh, while JoBeth Williams portrayed wife Revé.

Soon thereafter—some accounts claim the very next morning—Ottis Toole confessed to kidnapping and killing Adam Walsh. Hollywood police seemed confident the case was solved, then just as quickly pulled a turnabout, dismissing Toole as a suspect. The story of Toole's waffling statements on the boy's murder became a saga in itself, but after first proclaiming Toole the slayer, officers were steadfast in opining that he simply craved publicity. Over the years to come, by means still unexplained, the Hollywood P.D. managed to "lose" most of the meager evidence collected between 1981 and '83, including the 1971 Cadillac in which Toole once claimed he'd sodomized and murdered Adam Walsh.

John Walsh observed that travesty of justice from a distance, having moved on to a job with Fox Television, hosting *America's Most Wanted,* a series profiling fugitives at large and missing persons. The show premiered on February 7, 1988, and four days later led directly to the capture of an FBI "Top Ten" fugitive, an

Indiana serial killer sought by police for ten months. Before its cancellation in October 2012, the program aired 1,186 episodes and resulted in the capture of 1,200 fugitives.

Meanwhile, at Raiford, Gerard Schaefer sat with Toole and hatched what he regarded as a brilliant scheme. John Walsh had prospered from his son's demise. Why shouldn't Toole and Schaefer do the same?

Why not, indeed?

Schaefer wrote a letter, his penmanship unmistakable to any of his correspondents, later claiming that Toole "dictated" its contents. Lacking a home address for the Walshes, he traced the Adam Walsh Center in West Palm Beach and sent his missive there, addressed to John. It caught up with Walsh in an airport, hand delivered by longtime friend Les Davies. Postmarked from Starke prison at Raiford, it read:

> Dear Walsh:
>
> I'm the person who snatched, raped and murdered & cut up the little prick teaser, Adam Walsh, and dumped his smelly ass into the canal. You know the story but you don't know where his bones are. I do.
>
> Now you are a rich fucker, money you made from the dead body of that little kid. Oh, he was

a sweet piece of ass! I want to make a deal with you. Here's my deal. You pay me money and I'll tell you where the bones are so you can get them buried all decent and Christian.

I know you'll find a way to make sure I get the electric chair but at least I'll have money to spend before I burn. If you want the bones of your little cock teaser you send a private lawyer with money for me. No cops, no State Attorneys. No FDLE. Just a private lawyer with a written contract. I get $5,000 as "good faith" money. Then when I show you some bones I get $45,000. You get a lawyer to make up a paper like that.

If you send the police after me before we make a deal then you don't get no bones and what's left of Adam's hot pussy can rot. I remember how the little bitch was crying for his mommy when I was ramming his asshole. I love to fuck a boy, and then I love to kill them. Now you want his bones or not? Tell the cops and you don't get shit.

Sincerely, Ottis E. Toole

It goes without saying that Walsh paid Toole nothing. Instead, after vomiting, he sent four copies of the letter to the Hollywood Police Department, where—as stated in his 1997 memoir, *Tears of Rage*—"those dumb sons of bitches" failed to place even a single copy in their murder case file. Years later, in January 1996, Walsh and his wife gave another copy to Michael J. Satz, state attorney for the Seventeenth Judicial District, including Broward County. That time, they took along four witnesses, so Satz could not deny receiving it. Aghast at what he read, Satz told Walsh, "A jury would convict a man on the basis of this letter alone."

But it was not to be. As we shall see, no charge was ever filed in Adam's case, and Hollywood P.D. waited another 12 years before pronouncing Toole—long dead by then—definitively guilty in the case. So Adam's case was "cleared" without a single court appearance, though the controversy over what became of him continues to the present day.

Before all that, Walsh learned of Schaefer's role in the affair. As he laid out his knowledge of the incident in *Tears of Rage,*

> As it turned out, Toole had
> dictated the letter to a cellmate
> who could write, a guy named

Gerard Schaefer, a former state trooper [*sic*] who had been convicted for a series of rapes and murders. For a while there, the two had a little cottage industry going, writing letters all over the place, trying to extort money for alleged "information." They were all the same. Long on ghoulish detail. No hard proof.

While granting that Walsh's information on Schaefer, name aside, was false, what should we make of the "cottage industry" remark? So far, no other cases have been publicized, no victims named. It seems Schaefer and Toole also avoided any discipline in prison for tormenting Walsh, although a pair of sergeants from the Broward County Sheriff's Department *did* follow up by interviewing Schaefer in 1988. After their visit, Hollywood P.D. Chief Dick Witt received a memo from Detective Jack Hoffman, in charge of Adam's case, reporting that "Gerald [*sic*] Schaefer informed them that Ottis Toole told him that he used a bayonet to commit the Walsh Murder."

Police could find the weapon, Schaefer stated, hanging over the mantel at the home of Toole's sister, Vinetta Cipers. Officers stopped by her house and found the knife in question, but Cipers said she had owned it since 1979. She granted officers permission to run forensic tests on the weapon, but never learned the results. Following those tests, Detective Hoffman filed another report saying, "There is no evidence at this time to link Ottis Toole to the Walsh Murder."

In 1997, after *Tears of Rage* was published, new Hollywood P.D. Chief Rick Stone ordered a reexamination of the case. From that review, Stone said he now had evidence proving "beyond a reasonable doubt" that Toole killed Adam Walsh. By that time, Toole was dead, and thus could not defend himself, much less be charged with anything. Before year's end, according to John Walsh, a lab at Gainesville's University of Florida tested five knives linked to Toole for microscopic striations matching marks on Adam's vertebrae. They eliminated four, but found the sister's bayonet "not inconsistent" with the severed head's wounds.

Despite that finding, 11 more years slipped away before yet another police chief— Chadwick Wagner, a friend of John Walsh— officially closed Adam's case on December 16, 2008, declaring that an "external review" of the files left him convinced of Toole's guilt. In fact, Wagner told journalists, Toole had been his department's prime suspect "all along," even during the years when department spokesmen flatly denied Toole's involvement. Granting that mistakes were made by his department over time, Wagner apologized to Adam's family, and John

Walsh accepted, saying, "We can now move forward knowing positively who killed our beautiful little boy."

Had Schaefer lived to see that day, he doubtless would have been convulsed by laughter in his cell.

Chapter 9: Killer "Fiction"

Schaefer lost an admirer on January 24, 1989, when Ted Bundy kept his long-delayed appointment with Old Sparky. Two weeks later, on February 8, he got a new lease on life in the form of a letter from ex-girlfriend Sandy Stewart —now Sondra London, a desktop publisher styling herself the "Media Queen." Since dumping the Hangman in 1965, she'd graduated near the top of her class at Stranahan High, married a calypso band leader and bore him a daughter before they divorced, worked as a paralegal, designed software flow charts for the space shuttle, then settled in Atlanta as a freelance technical writer. Shocked by Schaefer's arrests and convictions, she'd waited 16 years before writing him to ask, "Do you remember me?"

"How could I *not* remember you?" the Hangman answered, and just like that, they were off to the races. London had read Ann Rule's memoir of friendship with Ted Bundy, *The Stranger Beside Me* (1980), and saw potential profit in her past relationship with Schaefer. Gerard, for his part, had long dreamed of publishing his graphic tales of mayhem for a large, paying audience. Other writers had approached him, Schaefer said, but he was "favorably disposed toward someone who has known me intimately." They struck a deal, later a grim bone of contention that would end with litigation and death threats. In 1989, however, all seemed to be sweetness and light—or sweetness and *dark,* considering Schaefer's thoughts set to paper.

Sondra was surprised at her first meeting with Schaefer since 1965. Instead of the tall, smiling blonde with "movie-star good looks" and a deepwater tan, she saw a portly, pale, slump-shouldered convict, balding and peering half-blind through thick spectacles. Overall, he struck her as a "middle-aged, desk-bound clerk gone to seed." Nothing had tamed his wits though, much less his Grand Guignol eye for gory and lascivious detail. Between March and May 1989, Schaefer sent London seven grisly tales with titles such as "Cut Bait," "Murder 101," and "Death House Screams." Some featured fictional detective Dan Kelly—based on real-life Detective David Kelly of the North Miami Beach P.D.—on paper a "rogue cop" who murders prostitutes in his spare time. London added drawings and fragments of writing seized from Doris Schaefer's home in 1973, self-publishing the lot in June 1989 as *Killer Fiction.*

Sales-wise, it tanked. So did a sequel, *Beyond Killer Fiction,* released in 1991 with stories including "Blonde on a Stick," "Flies in Her Eyes," "Gator Bait," and "Jesse in Flames."

Schaefer tossed in some half-baked philosophy under the heading "Being Called Ghoulish," concluding that the label didn't fit him, since "nobody has found anything on me that came off a corpse."

That much, again, was technically correct —but detectives had found *plenty* of dead women's relics, including souvenirs and gold-filled teeth, at Doris Schaefer's home in 1973. Of course, the Hangman swore Jack Dolan left them there.

*****

A major paradox quickly emerged from Schaefer's letters to London, placed in the public domain as federal court evidence in 1993. On one hand, he claimed to be innocent, framed by drug-dealing cops and prosecutors who feared his integrity, casting himself in a martyr's role. "I let Satan get control of me," he wrote. "I hated Evil. I wanted to destroy Evil. I went and immersed myself in the battle but destroyed myself in the process. God saved me by allowing me to be framed by corrupt people." A week later, he added, "My battle has been to overcome the problem [of serial killing]. I believe I have accomplished this through Jesus Christ. My own personal belief in Jesus...assures me of my future as a child of God, but that does not excuse me from helping my fellow man." That "help" apparently consisted of writing graphic murder tales for sale. Not that money mattered. "My reward, if any," Schaefer wrote, "will be a spiritual one."

The flip side of that angelic posture was Schaefer's gloating description of his ongoing role in organized crime. On March 15, 1989, he wrote to London

> I am known as a co-owner of prime hemp land in Belize. Our product is "Sinsemilla Royale." I'm KNOWN as an OWNER...I WALKED THE YARD with George T[r]aber and while that may mean absolutely less than nothing to you in prison that is a ticket to acceptability into the most exalted criminal ranks. I was Traber's "legal eagle" which is akin to being the Consigliere to a Godfather in New York...AND I got Traber out on escape...
>
> I live by the laws of the Criminal Underworld, and what is called the Convict Code. I wipe my ass on the Florida Statutes, the U.S. Code. I have become, as a matter of necessity and survival, a master criminal...

I am *not* of your society anymore. I am of the criminal underworld. My word is my bond. Your society does not understand that anymore...If you betray my trust I can, *if* I choose, have you and your kid dead at the bottom of the Chattahoochee river within 30 days. Such matters take longer when I can't get near a phone...

My sister was raped. The rapist was dealt with. A man threatened my step-father. He spent 4 days bound & gagged in a closet and his house was robbed of every thing in it. I don't fuck around. Mess with my family and you get hurt.

And six days later:

I am, at this time, enmeshed in a world of boundless evil. I am, factually, a captain in the Dixie Mafia; (I joke about it, but it's not really a funny matter)...I have, factually, the power to have you killed. I have, in the past, used these powers...

True Story: About 1983 my dad had to come up with

131

$12,500 or lose his house. A certain Crime Boss sent a person to him one day with a check for $12,500 to pay off the debt, and he was told verbally, ["]This is a gift. It need not be paid back.["] My dad was *shocked* to his soul. He kept after me, ["]I got to pay the money back. People don't give away $12,500 to an old man!!!["] Oh, but they do, Dad. In my world. My mom receives a check every month for several hundred dollars to supplement her retirement. Compliments of the Syndicate. She's the mother of a sub-chief. Her life should be eased a bit where possible...Tribute from the Underworld. I am loyal, after all. See?

And again, on March 24:

I *am* a Syndicate man, not the Mafia, of course, but my Boss has associations to the Mafia people...I took the proverbial "offer one can't refuse" and was never sorry about it for a minute...When I put on my O/C [organized crime] subchief's hat I

am "Don El Tigre" (my handle in
the life) and I can scare this [*sic*]
shit out of you...

And so on. As always, Schaefer wanted to
have it both ways: he was both a Christian
"saved" by Jesus, guaranteed a place in Heaven,
and a ravening monster. One letter, dated January
18, 1991, ghoulishly mingled both themes.

I'll tell you an absolutely confidential
story here...There were some young
women who were about to die. They were
already naked for the slaughter.
Frightened and out of their wits naturally.
I fed on their fear—rather the evil entity
did—and as I walked over to this one to
kill her she said to me: ["]Jesus loves you
and so do I.["] It was as if a sheet of glass
came down between us. She was as close
to dying as 5 seconds and everything
stopped. Frozen frame. I recall taking
several steps back. I recall it absolutely.
Then another woman, she was about to be
killed to[o]; she said, "No, nobody could
love him, not even God could love him." I
walked over to where she was laying on
her back and looked down into her eyes
and saw her hate. I killed her. It was
bloody and efficient. Then I killed the
rest. The one who'd called out the name of

133

Jesus died quickly, mercifully. That was the ONLY time in the career of the greatest SK [serial killer] of them all that he ever faltered after the woman was naked for the slaughter.

On January 18, 1991, Schaefer proposed marriage to London, noting that his wife could not be forced to testify against him "even if I were to show you a basket of severed heads." One day later, he reconsidered, scolding her for "abandoning" him in 1965 and, so he said, touching off his string of homicides.

Or had she? In one of Schaefer's stories, titled "First Kill," he dates the start of his murder spree from spring break of 1962, when, as he wrote, "I had just turned sixteen." Later in that same tale, he says, "In 1962 and 1963 I concentrated almost exclusively on transient hitch-hikers."

Was it confession, or pure imagination? It hardly mattered.

Schaefer's relationship with London went downhill from there.

*****

By 1991, the once and present partners had seen *Killer Fiction* and its sequel sink without a ripple in the literary marketplace. London was short on cash and Schaefer's lurid output failed to remedy that situation. The Hangman labeled his writing as "art," while Sondra held her peace and authorities branded the stories a blueprint for murder, thinly masking actual crimes in the guise of entertainment.

And Schaefer waffled on. While claiming he was innocent of any crime and "framed," he still couldn't resist flaunting his reputation as a serial killer. On April 7, 1989, he wrote: "As I see it, there are two ways to write the book. Should I prevail in Court, the book tells the tale of a cop victimized by corrupt officials. Should I ultimately lose in Court then the book takes a different slant...[M]y general theme would be the renditions of the 34 murders known and x-number unknown...I'd have no problem giving you '34 victims'."

Which victims, since neither 34 nor any number near that total had been named?

He began four days later, with Peggy Rahn and Wendy Stevenson. "So you say I killed Peggy & Wendy? OK. Fine. Now let's talk about *how* they died...I'll come up with something real horrible, bet that."

And so he did, on April 19, writing:

Peggy & Wendy just happened along at a time I was curious about [1930s cannibal Albert] Fish's craving for the flesh of young girls...and along comes two little Grace Budd types [a Fish victim]—young and tender—and solicit a ride. I assure you those girls were *not* molested sexually. I found them both very satisfactory, particularly with sautéed onions and peppers...I always had campers drift over to try my fare. Passed it off as wild game for the most part. Once a girl gets over 25 she's a bit tough and stringy.

He soon moved on to other crimes, sometimes still casting them as fiction, later dropping the façade. After first claiming he was in South Dakota in October 1966, when Mary Briscolina and Elsie Farmer vanished, Schaefer wrote (on April 27, 1989): "Of course, if I don't get out, I'll be glad to confirm that Mary Alice was a lovely girl, she sucked cock like a wet dream, so nicely in fact that I let her decide whether she or Elsie Lina should be strangled first."

A fantasy? Perhaps. And yet, two years later—on April 9, 1991—he wrote this concerning his tale "Murder Demons": "What crimes am I supposed to confess? Sykes? Farmer? Briscolina? What do you think Murder Demons is? Fiction? You want 'confessions' but you don't recognize them when I anoint you with them and we've just gotten started."

For the record, no victim named Sykes has yet been publicly linked to the Hangman.

He would also address Place and Jessup—albeit obliquely, while still claiming innocence of their deaths—in two items of "Killer Verse" titled "Suzie Prime True Crime" and "Georgia Peach," the latter describing Georgia "running toward the killing tree with Suzie." And then, there's the "Killer Art" he sent to London at Halloween 1991. His drawing depicts a nude woman lashed to a cross, severed head levitating above her blood-drenched neck and shoulders. In the margin, Schaefer wrote:

> She went looking for her head and
> somehow wound up dead. To fix
> the blame we really try. Evidence
> we falsify. One again I do repeat: I
> did not slay Miss Maggot Meat.

Ottis Toole liked that one so much that he scrawled his own marginalia, reading, "Cut me off a slice!"

On January 20, 1991, Schaefer wrote to London, "I am the top SK and I can prove it...As you know I've always harped on Stone's list of 34. In 1973 I sat down and drew up a list of my own. As I recall, my list was just over 80...I was the best." He raised the ante one day later, writing: "I'm not claiming a huge number...I would say it runs between 80 and 110. But over eight years and three continents...One whore drowned in her own vomit while watching me disembowel her girlfriend. I'm not sure that counts as a valid kill. Did the pregnant ones count as two kills? It can get confusing."

Confusing indeed. In another letter, he suggested "more than 175" victims killed and awaiting discovery.

*****

When not busy taunting, titillating, and threatening Sondra London, Schaefer still schemed to overturn his murder convictions. On September 18, 1990, he was back in court, pleading for a new trial. This time, he blamed Elton Schwartz for selling him out, presumably so that Schwartz could safely wed and bed Schaefer's then-wife Teresa. In legalese, presented by Federal Public Defender Kathleen Mary Williams, that meant a complaint of "ineffective counsel" based on Schwartz's sexual desire. On the witness stand, Schwartz said he had dissuaded Teresa from divorcing Schaefer earlier because "I felt, as Mr. Schaefer's attorney, that it would be devastating for his defense."

The whole arrangement reeked, but Schaefer couldn't catch a break. The court denied his motion and he went back home to Starke—where writing for his ex-girlfriend was growing hazardous. Once *Killer Fiction* made its tiny splash, prison guards began intercepting mail between Schaefer and London. When she sent him an advance copy of the book, hot off the press, an officer confiscated the tome, calling it "pornographic filth" which he deemed "unsuitable for a prisoner." It was eventually returned, but only after Florida Attorney General Bob Butterworth acknowledged that Schaefer's writings were related to a pending appeal.

In May 1991, guards struck again. The report reads: "At 9:30 a.m. of May 16, 1991...I opened a letter in front of Inmate Schaefer and discovered the envelope contained two letters discussing new stories to be written and other intended characters and plot. The letter and contents were turned over to Institutional Inspector Brian Gross and this report was written." As a result, Schaefer drew 30 days in solitary for "conspiracy to conduct a business from his cell."

Out in the free world, there was more turmoil to come.

Chapter 10: Poised to Sue Everyone

By summer 1991, Schaefer's working relationship with Sondra London was a train wreck waiting to happen. She couldn't support his "True Story" claims of a frame-up, although certain players in the drama were distinctly shady, and with his several confessions in hand, London prepared to try another route, but Schaefer wasn't buying it. On August 7, he wrote:

> I've repeatedly told you that I will not agree to anything in which I am portrayed as a SK. You are to *STOP* referring to me as a SK...You want me to say I'm an SK so you can make money from the lie. I went along with the KBS ["killer bullshit"] to help you sell books but there's a limit. I'm in U.S. Court, my case is before the 11th Circuit and you want me to go on ACA [TV's *A Current Affair*] and be touted as a SK. Are you *insane*? No, I think it's just greed.

And one week later, on the same theme: "I've told you time and time again not to refer to me as a serial killer. You've left the zone of reality and gone into your personal fantasyland and that *sucks*."

And again, on August 20: "I've received your letter of August 15. You violated both the wording and spirit of our agreement when you inserted unauthorized material into KF [*Killer Fiction*]. There is no doubt in my mind that you made that move in an effort to embarrass my family and ruin my habeas corpus litigations in U.S. Court. What you've done constitutes a personal betrayal and treachery of the meanest sort, and I'm not surprised you want to discontinue our project."

So far, his complaints might have seemed reasonable, had the Hangman himself not confessed to specific murders while speculating on a body count of 80 to more than 175 victims. As it was, he just sounded ridiculous.

Two months later, on November 17, Schaefer reversed himself, writing: "I can see where you're having money problems so I'm gonna give you a chance to make some cash...Go to ACA and get your fee...I'll cooperate...Let's quit bickering and go out and make money!"

If only it were that easy.

A Current Affair was a TV "news magazine"—tabloid style—that aired in syndication from 1986 to 1996. London told her story to reporter Steve Dunleavy, an Australian native whose shock-jock style inspired actor Robert Downey Jr.'s performance as character Wayne Gale in Oliver Stone's film *Natural Born Killers*. Around year's end, the segment aired, with London pulling no punches. Schaefer had been "normal" in high school, she said, "except for his compulsion to kill." As for the missing women, he had told her, "If there was no body, there was no crime. He said he would take a woman out into the Everglades and she'd be alligator meat by morning." Dunleavy signed off the segment by saying, "We can only pray that Gerard Schaefer can find his hell on Earth."

By January 15, 1992, Schaefer hadn't seen the program, but he wrote to London, "ACA: I can't really comment...reactions are coming in... [and] they are 100% of the opinion that ACA trashed me." Three months later, after finally watching a tape of the show, he wrote again.

> I saw ACA...and we're through. I don't even have to tell you another word, do I? I'm not gonna argue legalities with you. I'm just gonna ask you to be a nice lady and pack up everything GJS into some boxes. Seal them and send them to Mom... I want to be nice about this break so there are no evil feelings between us because if I get evil I'm

gonna come after you and ruin you...You let me know right away because if we're gonna fight I'm coming after your ass first...If you so much as sell one more KF or even mention my name in connection to an interview or the printed word or anything else I'll come after you and hound you into your grave and never quit. *You'll* become my life's work...How I feel about ACA's presentation transcends mere anger. You've tapped a Black Hole of genuine rage and it's focused on *you*.

In case London missed the point, Schaefer wrote, "I've trained myself to learn how to fight a legal war instead of asking one of the dudes from the Satan's Disciples Nation [a motorcycle gang] to arrange something violent. I'm on the very worst FSP population wing with the baddest of the bad but I help the nigs with their legal shit and that gets me accepted. Quite a few of these dudes are with gangs and I've got some good contacts to Yankee urban gangs such as the Vice Lords, the Latin Kings, El Ruken [*sic*], and Satan's Disciples Nation."

Schaefer's list of enemies expanded in a letter dated February 19, 1992. "If I lose in US Court," he wrote, "I'm gonna have Schwartz,

Teresa & Dean crippled. Arms and legs." Unless he used Teresa's maiden name by accident, the "Dean" remains mysterious.

Over the next four months, his letters turned chaotic, careening between vows of litigation and more threats of impending mayhem. His letter of April 24 merged both themes.

> I'm poised to sue everyone— articulately. I may not win but I'll break everyone's bank and make the lawyers richer...Then there is the matter of my being part of a separate society and our laws are different from your laws, all of which I explained to you in great detail. You seem to think I'm blowing hot air but I'm not. When I put things in gear shit happens. Why? Because I have the necessary criminal connections.

On May 12 he seemed to relent, writing, "I'll start by rescinding my prohibition against further sales of GJS writing. You just go ahead and do the orders that come in to you. I'll do the French interview. You come see me here and we'll talk over a film deal." But then, on June 19, he wrote, "My conscience is clear. Under Florida law you've abandoned our Agreement and I've fulfilled my legal obligation by offering you [*sic*] to revise it. You chose not to. The contract is broken and you've no claim; so please do not whore after me about it...The very next time you say or do anything that causes me problems...I am going to encourage my dope addled Satanist pals in Georgia to go pick up your slut daughter and teach her some sex education...My offer is simple: You don't fuck with me; I won't fuck with your kid."

Schaefer ultimately sued London three times (all dismissed) and tried to have her arrested for stealing his literary works "valued in excess of $110,000" (complaint likewise dismissed). London fought back, petitioning for a protective order, weighting her brief with 500 pages of Schaefer's death threats and murder confessions. Finally barred by prison authorities from writing to London directly, Schaefer penned a furious letter to her British publisher on December 5, 1993. In that florid missive he wrote: "My closest associate in this slimepit is an Anointed Fourth Prince of the Hand of Death who was a contract killer for the Mafia...This man has gunned down mobsters from Miami to New York...All I need to do is ask the gentleman to have SL and her kid murdered and it would be done. SL is alive at this moment because I choose to allow it."

*****

How, you may ask, does a convict serving life for multiple murders sue anyone in the free world, including total strangers? The simple answer is: it's easy. They learn sufficient rudiments of legalese to scrawl a semi-literate brief, file it with their court of choice, and dodge most normal fees by claiming poverty. Under state and federal law, the courts are obliged to carry out service of summons and hear each case, at least to a point.

"Score Card Killer" Randy Steven Kraft set the standard for frivolous lawsuits in May 1993 when he accused his unauthorized biographer, Dennis McDougal, of libeling him in the book *Angel of Darkness* (1991). Despite his conviction for killing and mutilating 16 young men, which landed him on San Quentin's death row, Kraft sought $62 million in damages, claiming McDougal had not only smeared his "good name" and portrayed him as a "sick, twisted man...without moral values," but also "destroyed his chances for future employment." California's Supreme Court dismissed the case in June 1994, but by that time, Schaefer had raised the fallen torch.

*****

He was distracted briefly when Sondra London returned to Starke in February 1993—but not to see the Hangman. This time, the object of her attention was "Gainesville Ripper" Daniel Harold

146

Rolling, sentenced to die for the August 1990 murders of five college students, suspected of at least three more slayings in his native Louisiana. Together, London and Rolling would produce a book titled *The Making of a Serial Killer* (1996), but their relationship went further still. As she told the *New York Times* on February 24, "I got a letter today proposing marriage. I had written him making the same suggestion. Our letters crossed in the mail." Starke's chaplain, she said, was trying to arrange the ceremony—which later fell through.

Schaefer quickly learned the news through cellblock scuttlebutt and sent London a St. Valentine's Day card on February 13. It read, in part:

> Hello Whore, the word on the yard is that the Queen of the Sluts was at FSP romancing Danny Rolling. Word also has it that Bobby Lewis is ratting on the slut's main squeeze to the cops. The entire prison is aware of it: Bobby Lewis and Sondra London are taking down Rolling. Dude name of Williams says the whore is sexually mesmerizing Danny Boy while her pal, Lewis, pumps him and runs to the cops every time Danny opens his mouth. I was so

right about you, Sondra: *whore*. Pure fucking whore. A whore and a rat...Valentine, you're *mine*. Why you out front licking Danny's ego? I know what you're up to: *money*. You're gonna get Danny Boy fried while you make a buck off his misery. Right? Well, go for it! Just be sure you keep my name out of this episode. Should I find out that you say I'm a SK or see my name involved in any of this Rollings [*sic*] crap you're at the center of then I'm going to put you and your whoredaughter on my list of unfinished business. Williams don't like you worth shit and he claims to have KKK connections.

Rolling's short-lived engagement to London soon fizzled. He was executed by lethal injection—not "fried"—on October 25, 2006, leaving a confession to his suspected crimes in Louisiana. In May 2007, Florida Attorney General Bill McCollum Jr. filed a lien against Rolling's property and all earnings from *The Making of a Serial* killer under the state's "Son of Sam" Law, forbidding felons—even those deceased, apparently—from earning any profit off their crimes.

*****

Patrick Kendrick was among the Hangman's first litigation targets. A firefighter and paramedic turned freelance author, he was drawn to Schaefer's case and spent five years poring over files, conducting interviews, and corresponding with Schaefer, planning a book titled *Bloodlaw*. One day, after *A Current Affair* revived Robert Stone's claims that Schaefer was "one of America's worst serial killers ever," a supposed "young writer" wrote to Kendrick, asking if Schaefer had truly killed more than 40 women. Thinking back to headlines from 1973. Kendrick replied, "The number is not 'more than 40,' but 36, I believe." When the letter's author professed fear of meeting Schaefer in the flesh, Kendrick wrote, "Don't be. He is now a middle-aged, pale and doughy, bookish kind of wimp."

Alas, the supposed "young writer" was a free world crony of the Hangman, who passed Kendrick's letter along to Starke. Next came a summons, announcing Schaefer's lawsuit for $500,000, with a warning that unless Kendrick replied, "your wages, money, and property may thereafter be taken without further warning from the Court."

Kendrick duly hired a lawyer, and by January 1994 he'd spent more than $6,000 holding the Hangman at bay. As the case dragged on, with Kendrick reduced to battling insomnia with sleeping pills, Schaefer wrote again to say: "I apologize to your wife and kiddies for disrupting their lifestyle, but really you should have considered them before you decided on a course of criminal conduct. What do you want to do, Kendrick? Compromise, or pay and pay and pay lawyers?" Around the same time, gloating, Schaefer bared his true motive to interviewer John Dorschner. Kendrick had insulted him, but now Schaefer was "showing him I'm not a wimp." At a long-distance mediation hearing in January 1994, Schaefer offered to settle for an unspecified "small amount," but Kendrick refused. Their trial was scheduled for March, but instead Kendrick agreed to give Schaefer one copy from his manuscript, listing alleged victims. That settled the case "with prejudice," meaning Schaefer couldn't sue again—but he did, twice more. The second lawsuit was dismissed, and a third was pending at Schaefer's death.

And so it went. Cheated of the sadistic pleasure he had once derived from hanging women, Schaefer had found another way to make his victims squirm. The jailhouse lawyer cherished an illusion of control over his enemies.

Another victim was Michael Cartel, who devoted a short chapter to Schaefer's case in *Disguise of Sanity: Serial Mass Murderers* (1985). On June 1, 1993, he received "a rambling several page letter" from Schaefer, addressed to "Legal Counsel" at Cartel's personal post office box. It began, "I am advised that your company is the publisher for Michael Cartel," and went on from there, demanding cash for sundry slurs against Schaefer's nonexistent "good name." As Cartel explained in a blog, 22 years later, "I wrote back that I would not reward him. A second letter from Schaefer arrived on July 8, saying he would give me 15 days to submit to all his demands before filing a suit against me in Florida, where (he said) the climate of a libeled plaintiff is much more favorable. That's the last I heard from him." At that, he was lucky.

Meanwhile, Schaefer *did* file lawsuits against various others, including forensic dentist Richard Souviron, who identified Carmen Hallock's teeth in 1973, later providing photos and snippets of Schaefer's writings to a British magazine; former FBI agent Robert Ressler, for describing Schaefer's case in *Whoever Fights Monsters* and citing the Hangman in his traveling slide show on serial killers; *Globe* supermarket tabloid, for an article asserting Schaefer was "connected to 34 dead and missing girls"; author Jay Robert Nash, for briefly summarizing Schaefer's case in his *World Encyclopedia of 20th Century Murder* (1992), itself a fragment of the much longer, error-ridden *Encyclopedia of World Crime* (1990); Dr. Joel Norris, for garbling Schaefer's resumé in *Serial Killers: The Growing Menace* (1988); and Anne Schwartz, for an appendix in her book on Jeffrey Dahmer, *The*

Man Who Could Not Kill Enough (1992), listing various killers and crediting Schaefer with "20+" murders. That appendix was written by Dr. Ronald Holmes, a professor of criminology at the University of Kentucky, so Schaefer naturally sued Holmes and wrote to the university, demanding that Holmes be fired to defer litigation.

When Schaefer went transatlantic, suing British author Colin Wilson for including his case in *The Serial Killers: A Study in the Psychology of Violence* (1991), he hit a brick wall. The court dismissed his case, while ruling that the Hangman's loathsome reputation was "libel proof" under the law. Wilson later wrote the foreword to a new edition of *Killer Fiction,* saying that Schaefer was afflicted with "halitosis of the soul."

And then, there was the Hangman's case against Yours Truly.

*****

I arrived late in Schaefer's world, having missed his case entirely during 1972-73. While researching my book *Hunting Humans: An Encyclopedia of Serial Killers* (1990), I found him mentioned briefly in the *New York Times* and in *Serial Killers,* by the late Joel Norris. What resulted was a 101-word entry, reading as follow:

A homicidal ex-policeman from Oakland Park, Florida, dubbed the "Sex Beast" by local newsmen, Schaefer was theoretically linked with the murders of at least 20 persons after the jewelry, teeth, and clothing of several victims were recovered from a trunk in the attic of his mother's home. The public defender's office was unable to prevent Schaefer's conviction and imprisonment on first-degree murder charges, but the killer took it in stride. When Schaefer's wife divorced him and became engaged to his defense attorney, he gave the couple his blessing, requesting that the same lawyer continue to handle his case through forthcoming appeals.

I subsequently learned of two errors in that entry, both borrowed from a timeline of serial killers in Norris's book. First, Schaefer was never called "the Sex Beast," an appellation reporters actually applied to Melvin Davis Reese, a 1950s killer who died, imprisoned, in 1995. The other error was restricting Schaefer's crimes to Oakland Park. Such glitches, as I came to know, were commonplace in Dr. Norris's work, as in that of others.

Although released by a small press in Washington State, *Hunting Humans* caught fire after it was mentioned in a *New York Times Book Review* compendium of unusual reference books. Soon Avon Books, a major New York publisher (now owned by HarperCollins), purchased paperback rights and released the book as two mass-market volumes in 1992.

By then I was on Schaefer's radar, via correspondence with Sondra London. He mentioned me first in a letter to Sondra, dated July 20, 1990. Ten days later, after I acknowledged the errors inherited from Dr. Norris and apologized, he wrote: "Newton seemed sane and fair minded in his response. I'm wondering who started that Sex Beast crap? ...*Sex Beast* might be a great title for the True Story."

Soon I was corresponding directly with Schaefer himself, hearing his "True Story" of an innocent cop framed by colleagues. I was skeptical, yet on January 15, 1992, Schaefer wrote to London, "Mike Newton: I had a letter from him. Answered it. I think he is qualified to run with the TS so I'm tentatively agreeable." Two weeks later, he advised London, "If you want to do a TS about me then we'll come to some sort of contract agreement and do it. You, me, MN." Soon afterward, he must have caught the hint that I questioned his claims of innocence. On April 16, 12 days after his cease-and-desist order to London, he wrote to her: "Please contact

Mike Newton and have him return to you all the material you've sent him concerning myself and my case. You may send all that down to Mom along with the stuff you have about me now in your possession."

I received no such request, nor would I have indulged it, even though I had no further plans to write a book about the Hangman. I *did* mention him once more—a single sentence terming his murders "prolific"—in *Serial Slaughter* (1992), a sequel of sorts to *Hunting Humans* from the same publisher.

My notice of impending litigation came by mail in June 1993, as briefly described in the preface to *Hangman*. I was apprehensive of the cost at first, but Avon's editors very generously bore the financial weight, while I supplied documentary evidence in conjunction with Sondra London. Since Schaefer had filed with the U.S. District Court in Indianapolis, Avon hired the estimable firm of Barnes & Thornburg. The lead attorney on our case was Jan M. Carroll (presently a partner with the firm).

Schaefer had many legal balls in the air that summer and fall, but he followed each with the attentiveness of a malevolent god tracking vultures in flight. At one point, he filed an ethics complaint against Ms. Carroll for "violating doctor-patient confidentiality." Her alleged offense: submitting Schaefer's psychiatric test results as evidence. I was on the phone with Jan when she received the complaint, and I could feel her anger simmering over the long-distance line. In an effort to calm her, I said, "He's sitting in his cell right now, laughing because he's ruined your day." She pushed on, aware that Sondra London had published the psych reports as an informational handout in 1989, and the peevish complaint was dismissed.

When he drew my case in 1993, Judge Steckler—Indiana born in 1913 and appointed to the federal bench in 1950 by President Harry Truman—was nearing retirement. In fact, death from non-Hodgkin lymphoma awaited him, less than 22 months from the date *Schaefer v. Newton and Avon Books* was filed, but he would see it through and hand the Hangman a stinging defeat in the end.

Between filing his case and year's end, Schaefer learned of *Serial Slaughter* and began to draft a second action, this one to be heard in Florida as an added inconvenience to me. On December 20, 1993, he sent me an ironic Christmas card. Its face bore the message "Thoughts of you bring special memories," imposed over a snowy rural scene. Inside, the card went on: "Thanking God for you...for the blessing you are...for the joys you bring! May your Christmas be special in every way." The *real* message, however, appeared in Schaefer's unmistakable block printing.

Seasons Greetings!
Would you like to start the New Year off without any legal stuff? Why don't you settle up with me[?] Take me out of your books, don't tell anyone lies about me being a serial killer, make me a compensatory settlement. That's the easy way. I'll even forgo filing the new suit against you I have drawn up. Do you have a lawyer in Florida? It's your money, Mike, and I intend to stay on you permanently. I don't quit when someone does me wrong. Here's your chance to make a fair settlement. Don't ever say that I have a greedy wicked heart. Not me! So what do you say?

I said nothing, and he filed the second case in Florida as promised, titled *Schaefer v. Newton and Loompanics Unlimited*. Once again, I was spared the cost of hiring counsel, and a jurist who knew the Hangman well dismissed the case. Schaefer, of course, appealed.

Back in Indianapolis, Judge Steckler issued his ruling on July 11, 1994. After deciding that my *Hunting Humans* entry was predominately true, written and published without malice, Steckler went on to say:

157

The truth of this case may or may not be that Schaefer is responsible for the deaths of scores of his fellow humans. The depravity which inheres in such conduct is self-evident. What is also evident is that Schaefer is a self-proclaimed serial killer genius and that he is a convicted double-murderer. This latter fact makes him a serial killer as that term is defined by Newton and others. Schaefer can quarrel with this definition, but only by arguing that it should be changed. The record establishes beyond doubt that Schaefer has indeed been linked to the murders of at least 20 persons. The recovery of items referred to in the first sentence of the entry is a matter of public record. He boasts of the private and public associations he has had based on the reports that he is a serial killer of world-class proportions and it is only arrogant perversity which propels him toward this and similarly meritless lawsuits.

Steckler awarded court costs to Avon. Schaefer lost his appeal of Judge Steckler's verdict in June 1995. Case closed.

Back at Starke, while threatening others, the Hangman had survival issues of his own. In November 1994, while drafting an appeal of his second suit against me, he suffered serious injuries. As he told the appellate court on November 11: "While working in the prison law library Plaintiff was attacked by another inmate and stabbed repeatedly in and about the face, body and hands. Due to the trauma sustained incidental to this attack, Plaintiff is now unable to prosecute his appeal; therefore Plaintiff withdraws the appeal in this case."

Things quickly went from bad to worse, as Danny Rolling informed Sondra London. Schaefer was having "big time problems" and was "on everyone's shit list" at Starke—literally. During the week before Rolling set pen to paper, prisoners pelted the Hangman with urine and feces, twice setting fire to his cell. Whatever papers didn't burn were doused and ruined by the cellblock's sprinkler system. Word was out, Rolling said, that Schaefer was "a manipulating *SNITCH* and has been for a long time."

But not for much longer.

*****

On December 4, 1995, I received notice from the U.S. Court of Appeals in Tallahassee that *Schaefer v. Newton and Loompanics* was dismissed "because appellant [Schaefer] has failed to pay the $100 docketing and $5 filing fees to the district court within the time fixed by the rules." In fact, Schaefer was long past paying any further fees, ever again. On Sunday, December 3, guards found the Hangman butchered in his twice-burnt cell, lying with his throat slashed, stabbed 42 times about his head and neck. (Posthumous rumors that his eyes had been carved out proved false.) Guards retrieved no weapon. A bloody handprint on the wall appeared to be the only clue. Schaefer's final photo, from the morgue, may be the only one in which he doesn't wear a smile. The Hangman's death discomfited Fort Lauderdale homicide detective Tim Bronson, who had reopened the Bonadies, Hallock, and Hutchins cases in autumn 1995. On December 1, 1995, Bronson had phoned Starke, making an appointment to interview Schaefer on Monday, December 4. But once again, the Hangman slipped away.

Chapter 11: Question Marks

Echoes of Schaefer's case continue more than 20 years beyond his death. Relieved from any threat of costly nuisance suits, Bill Haggerty, a former FBI agent who'd studied Schaefer for the Bureau's fledgling Violent Criminal Apprehension Program in the early 1980s, spoke openly at last, calling the Hangman "one of the sickest" serial killers on record. "If I had a list of the top five," Haggerty said, "which would include all of the serial killers I have interviewed throughout the country, he would definitely be in the top five."

Heedless of his crimes, or still convinced of Schaefer's innocence, his loved ones grieved. His sister, Sara Keen, told reporters, "Our mother hasn't stopped crying. And my daughter, who was only a child at the time, cried so much she broke out—she got a rash from crying so much."

For Shirley Jessup, still mourning daughter Georgia, Schaefer's death was simply a case of justice delayed. "I'd like to send a present to the guy who killed him," she told reporters. "I've always believed he was going to get his. I just wish it would have been sooner [rather] than later." Debora Lowe's mother missed Schaeffer's murder, having died on December 23, 1994, but the Hangman's slaying fell on her birthday. Surviving members of the Lowe family took the news as a sign from Heaven of their mother confirming that justice was done.

Families of the lost young women still wait in vain for relief. Ten days after Schaefer's murder, Fort Lauderdale's *Sun-Sentinel* ran an article headlined "Untangling Tortured Web of a Killer." The piece lamented that, with Schaefer's passing, "the secrets to the fates of dozens of women likely died too." Authors Scott Glover and Jaime Abdo specifically listed Leigh Bonadies, Carmen Hallock, Belinda Hutchins, Collette Goodenough, and Barbara Wilcox. "I believe he killed them all," they quoted Philip Shailer, Broward County's state attorney from 1969 to 1976. "Unfortunately," he continued, "with that evidence alone [from Doris Schaefer's home] you couldn't even get a case to the jury. Without some other evidence linking Schaefer to those girls, the law would not allow that leap of assumption. Ultimately, he got what he should have." As for Mary Briscolina and Elsie Farmer, detectives told the *Sun-Sentinel* they would keep those cases open "for a few weeks" in an effort "to at least let the victims' families know what happened."

The crimes remain officially unsolved today.

Fort Lauderdale police, meanwhile, were caught flat-footed in their scheme to charge

Schaefer with three unsolved murders, thereby ensuring he never made his 2017 parole date. At Starke, prison administrators took their time in solving Schaefer's murder—if, in fact, they ever did. On February 1, 1996, they charged Vincent Faustino Rivera, inmate No. 518548, already serving life plus 20 years for two murders committed in Hillsborough County. Rivera was angered, prosecutors claimed, by Schaefer taking the last hot water from a cellblock dispenser. When he protested, Schaefer allegedly replied that, if not for his efforts, there would have been no water heater on the block to start with. After brooding awhile, Rivera supposedly returned with a shank and gave Schaefer the treatment his unnumbered victims had suffered before him, furiously stabbing the Hangman and slashing his throat. Convicted of second-degree murder on June 8, 1999, Rivera received an additional term of 53 years and 10 months. His prospects for release are nil.

Between indictment and conviction, in November 1996, Rivera wrote to Sondra London, dismissing the case against him as a "Mickey Mouse" fabrication concocted by a convict desiring transfer to a better lockup. Rivera claimed that the bloody palm print from the Hangman's cell matched neither Schaefer's nor his own, and that the alleged murder weapon bore neither bloodstains nor fingerprints. If that were not enough, Rivera wrote, he never drank electrically heated water, because some prison nurse had warned that it would poison him.

Rivera named no alternate slayer, but Schaefer's mother fingered Ottis Toole as the murder's instigator. In her version, communicated to Sondra London via telephone on February 23, 1996, Toole had been dying of cancer (false) and had confided the location of Adam Walsh's burial site to Schaefer in November 1995. The Hangman, in turn, was allegedly negotiating with Hollywood P.D. Detective Mark Smith for his own prison transfer back to Avon Park, a *quid pro quo* for accommodating John and Revé Walsh, when Toole panicked and arranged Schaefer's death. That same story surfaced in a February 1996 issue of the tabloid *National Enquirer,* headlined "Killer Set to Reveal Adam Walsh's Fate is Murdered in Jail." According to that piece, Adam's parents were "sick at heart" over the loss of their potential benefactor.

Before cirrhosis of the liver claimed his life in September 1996, Toole once again retracted his public admission of the Walsh murder, although rumors persist of another confession to his niece in 1995 and/or a final deathbed statement to his sister, presently unproven. Whatever Toole said at the end, Schaefer's family missed the point that his involvement with the grisly Walsh extortion letter was no more than an expression of Gerard's malignant sadism.

As for the fabled book and film touted by Schaefer in his final interviews, destined to prove his innocence and set him free at last, neither has yet appeared. There is no reason to believe they ever will.

If Schaefer had survived, he doubtless would have sued crime writer Stephen Michaud and ex-FBI forensic profiler Roy Hazelwood for their collaboration on a book, *The Evil That Men Do,* in 1999. Hazelwood had referred to Schaefer's case earlier, in an article for the *FBI Law Enforcement Bulletin,* but wisely omitted Schaefer's name. In his new opus with Michaud, Hazelwood felt free to name the Hangman, crediting him with 29 suspected victims—and, incidentally, claiming that Florida headlines dubbed Schaefer "The Sex Beast." That error, in and of itself, would have produced a legal filing —as, no doubt, would the careless reversal of Schaefer's first and middle names in the book's index.

In July 2007, *Tampa Bay Times* reporter Kameel Stanley published an article headlined "41 Years Later, Killings Solved." The piece named Schaefer as the slayer of Nancy Leichner and Pam Nater in October 1966, based upon "a witness account and the recent discovery of long-mishandled confessions of the killer." Lake County sheriff's sergeant Ken Adams, head of a multicounty task force assigned to solve the double murder, told Stanley, "To be honest, it's a bittersweet satisfaction, because you don't know where the remains are." The witness in question was Brent Hoover, 11 years old in 1966, who was canoeing in the area when Pam and Nancy disappeared. Decades too late, Hoover identified Schaefer as the man whom he saw following the victims around the Ocala National Forest's Alexander Springs Recreation Area. As far as Schaefer's confession, that came from notes written by Charles Sizelove, an Avon Park inmate who served time with Schaefer in the early 1980s. Summarized by Stanley, said notes revealed how "Schaefer told Sizelove he took Leichner and Nater by gun and knifepoint and killed them." Strangely, Sizelove's writings never came to light while Schaefer lived, even after authorities requested them for an unrelated 1985 missing-person case.

Two years later, in July 2009, true crime author Arthur Jay Harris threw a monkey wrench into the state's solution of the Adam Walsh case with a self-published book titled *Jeffrey Dahmer's Dirty Secret: The Unsolved Murder of Adam Walsh*. Based on years of research, and coming seven months after the state's posthumous pseudo-conviction of Ottis Toole for killing the lost six-year-old, Harris revealed that infamous cannibal Dahmer was living in Florida when Adam vanished and working just 20 minutes distant from Hollywood Mall where the boy disappeared in July 1981. Furthermore, Harris named seven witnesses who identified Dahmer as the man they saw with or near Adam at the mall, including one who recalled Dahmer forcing the boy into a blue van outside. One composite sketch of the mustachioed suspect resembled Dahmer more than Toole, and his boss owned a blue van, available to all employees on request. Harris's account also referred to a police report on Dahmer "supposedly finding a dead body in an alley behind where he worked" prior to Adam's slaying. That report further described a meter and storage room nearby, where Harris and ABC News investigators allegedly found "blood droplets rising up a wall next to a lumberman's axe and a sledgehammer."

According to an article in Broward County's *Sun-Sentinel* newspaper, published in March 2010, a Hollywood detective had "pitched softball questions" to Dahmer about Adam's case, while feeding the killer homemade muffins. Between mouthfuls, Dahmer replied, "Nothing to do with it." Also quoted in the story was Hollywood Mall witness Janice Santamassino, who said, "Once I saw that picture of Dahmer, I said, 'That's him.' That's who I saw." Clutching her four-year-old daughter close after they nearly bumped into Dahmer, Santamassino added, "He just gave me a bad, uncomfortable feeling. It was spooky." Moments later, the mall's intercom blared out a call for the missing Adam. Other witnesses told of reporting a Dahmer look-alike suspect to Hollywood police headquarters, which failed to return their phone calls during the two weeks between Adam's abduction and discovery of his severed head in a Vero Beach canal. As late as 1996, witness Jennie Warren's statement was dismissed out of hand by state attorney's investigator Phil Mundy, when Warren failed to identify Ottis Toole from a photo lineup. Thinking back to the fateful day in July 1981, Warren said, "I wish my mind could take a picture, because it would be him: Dahmer."

Arthur Harris was not done rocking the state's canoe, however. In June 2013 he published Book 2 of his Dahmer exposé, titled *Jeffrey Dahmer's Dirty Secret: The Unsolved "Murder" of Adam Walsh*, with a subtitle: *Finding the Victim*. For those who missed the title's broad hints, Harris wasted no time cutting to the chase. He now believed—and cited evidence to indicate —that Adam Walsh, while certainly kidnapped in 1981, had not in fact been slain. His ammunition for that broadside consisted of missing law enforcement files, including any vestige of an autopsy report; the fact that neither John Walsh nor his wife had viewed their son's alleged remains, leaving that burden to a friend; and a photograph of the child's severed head, clearly showing an upper left incisor where Adam should have had none, based on recent photographs. Allegedly, aside from one family friend's I.D., the head was labeled Adam's solely on the basis of one filling in a lower molar—that, Harris says, without requesting Adam's dental records or consulting a forensic dentist.

So, if Dahmer was the kidnapper, what did he do with Adam Walsh? Harris had no idea until, as he described it to one interviewer, his "already dark story risks going into Bizarroville." That's no exaggeration, since Harris claims to be in contact with an adult male, living in Miami, who maintains that *he* is Adam Walsh. According to the story told by "A. W."—Harris's tag for the informant—he was snatched by Dahmer from Hollywood Mall at age six, then driven to a house in Miami Beach where he was abused and tortured for days before blacking out. Waking in a Miami hospital with total amnesia, he was later adopted by a Hispanic family "whose natural child was another Dahmer victim," and who suspected their foundling was Adam Walsh. Of course, they made no effort to alert Adam's parents.

Bizarre coincidence, or a total fabrication?

The most obvious question is how and why "A. W." survived abduction by Dahmer, who'd killed his first victim in Ohio three years earlier, at age 18, then slaughtered 16 more in Milwaukee between 1987 and 1991. Would Dahmer take a living victim to the hospital in 1981, particularly if he had already killed another young child in the same vicinity, as suspected by "A. W.'s" adoptive parents? It seems incredible, and Dahmer, having once denied involvement in the case, was murdered by another con in prison on November 28, 1994. A second inmate, wounded in the same assault, died two days later. The attacker's motive: "God told me to do it."

Harris tells us that "A. W." took his adoptive parents' surname and works today in the undescribed family business, somewhere in southern Florida. College educated but "under-employed," he never married and has no children of his own. After the *Dallas Herald* and network television reviewed Harris's first book, "A. W." reached out with his story and Harris began checking available facts. First, he obtained scans of fingerprints recovered from Adam Walsh's bedroom in 1981, "but their original quality wasn't very good." Police files *did* contain mitochondrial DNA test results from Revé Walsh, deemed "consistent" with DNA from a ground-up tooth of the severed head, but Harris claims "lab controls showed that those test results were contaminated and therefore had no comparative value whatsoever." John Walsh, meanwhile, allegedly resists a DNA swab to compare with "A. W."—who, as of yet, has never contacted the family directly. When "A. W." met with Hollywood detectives for an hour, Harris says, "They were polite to him, but did nothing, wrote no report, took no saliva swabs for DNA, no fingerprints." Finally, Harris asks rhetorically, "Even if there was one half of a half of a half of a percent [chance] that A. W. is Adam, shouldn't the Walshes agree to DNA testing?"

Perhaps. Then again, considering the slew of people who have claimed to be world-famous characters returning from the grave—Grand Duchess Anastasia Nikolaevna of Russia, Jesse James, Butch Cassidy, Billy the Kid, John Dillinger, George "Machine Gun" Kelly, Elvis Presley and so on—perhaps not. Some wounds never completely heal.

In September 2015, another self-published book appeared, titled *Frustrated Witness! The True Story of the Adam Walsh Case and Police Misconduct.* Author Willis Morgan joined the chorus touting Jeffrey Dahmer as the murderer, without suggesting that Adam survived into adulthood. A self-proclaimed eyewitness, who allegedly saw Dahmer in Radio Shack at the Hollywood Mall before Adam's kidnapping, Morgan writes, "This is the account of Adam Walsh's abduction and my attempts stretching across decades to find justice for him. As much as this book is a case for Jeffrey Dahmer being Adam's murderer, it is equally a study of how the Hollywood Police Department conducted the homicide investigation." A litany ensues of evidence mishandled, inconvenient witnesses ignored, and a 12-year delay between Ottis Toole's death and the state's final pronouncement of his guilt.

171

Of one thing, we are certain. Schaefer, having lived and worked in southern Florida since age 14, was permanently out of circulation at the time when Adam Walsh was snatched and killed —or not. His involvement in the case, writing the ghoulish ransom note to John Walsh on behalf of nearly illiterate pen pal Ottis Toole, served Schaefer's sadism and nothing else. He may or may not have decided Toole was guilty of the crime. And Toole, with an IQ around room temperature on a cool day, had already changed his story on the kidnapping so often, he may not have known, himself.

None of that matters now. Schaefer's enduring legacy is one of pain and loss, of degradation and obsession, coupled with a yen for self-destruction handed down from early childhood games in which he "always died." Why else would he allow two teenage victims to escape his clutches while he left to stand for roll call at the sheriff's office back in 1972? Two quick shots would have subdued them permanently. Once imprisoned for those crimes the state could prove, why else would he court cellblock retribution by ratting out fellow convicts, angering burly jailhouse lawyers, even making enemies in distant lockups with his mail-order sex scams? Despite his claims of friendship with drug lords and hitmen, outlaw bikers, Ku Klux Klansmen, and the Hand of Death satanic cult, when time ran out, the Hangman's mother and sister were his only living friends.

And finally, how many lives did he snuff out? Was it the 29 suspected by Roy Hazelwood, the 34 mentioned in Florida headlines, or the 80 to 175 or more Schaefer personally claimed in 1991, scattered across three continents? The answer to that question went with Schaefer to his grave.

Since his murder, other fiends have come along who made even the Hangman's highest estimate of homicides seem paltry: Dr. Harold Shipman of England, convicted of killing 218 patients and suspected in 32 other cases; Luis Garavito in Colombia, with 138 victims confirmed and up to 300 more suspected; Pedro López, the "Monster of the Andes," with 110 victims confirmed in three South American countries and 300-plus suspected; Japan's Miyuki Ishikawa, killer of 103 infants and suspected in another 66 cases; Daniel Camargo Barbosa, with 72 kills confirmed in Colombia and Ecuador, another 300-plus suspected; and Serhiy Fedorovich Tkach, from Ukraine, with 37 confirmed victims and 100-plus claimed. The list goes on, and also stretches back into the past, including Hungarian Countess Erzsébet Báthory, whose 17th-century diary listed 610 victims; French nobleman and sorcerer Gilles de Rais, who reportedly confessed 400 child murders in the 15th century; and Thug Behram, a member of the Kali cult in India, who admitted participating in 900 ritual homicides during the 1800s.

In short, Gerard Schaefer exaggerated mightily in calling himself "the world's #1 serial killer." He wasn't even close.

In retrospect, and for his requiem, we can do little more than quote a bit of children's doggerel from London, circa 1889, concerning one of Schaefer's spiritual forebears.

Jack the Ripper's dead
And lying on his bed.
He cut his throat
With Sunlight soap.
Jack the Ripper's dead.

Afterword

When I began research for *Hangman,* I contacted the Wilton Manors Historical Society in search of further information on alleged missing victims Bonnie Taylor and Patricia Wilson. The society's answer, long delayed, arrived a week after the book's publication online, and while their files contained no information on the vanished women, Secretary Benjamin Little dropped a bombshell concerning Schaefer's dismissal from the local police force. FBI agents and others speculate that Schaefer was fired for harassing women whom he met on traffic stops, but Mr. Little writes that "Schaefer was hired in September 1971 and fired in April 1972 for hanging a (drunk?) man upside down under a bridge. Schaefer's subsequent history caused our police chief, Bernard Scott to institute psychological testing for all new hires."

No other journalist involved with Schaefer's case from 1972 to the present day has discovered this news, which paints a distinctly darker portrait of Schaefer in Wilton Manors, his aberration reaching far beyond the level of an officer who simply "had no common sense." Had he been prosecuted and incarcerated for the mock lynching in spring 1972, multiple murder victims slain while he awaited trial and sentencing in Martin County might still be alive today.

Again, the Hangman managed to evade justice and go about his killing undeterred.

Thank you to my editor, proofreaders, and cover artist for your support:

~ **Michael Newton**

Aeternum Designs (book cover), Bettye McKee (editor), Lee Knieper Husemann, Lorrie Suzanne Phillippe, Marlene Fabregas, Darlene Horn, Ron Steed, Katherine McCarthy, Robyn MacEachern, Kathi Garcia, Linda H. Bergeron

About the Author

Hangman is Michael Newton's 307th published book since 1977. His history of the Florida Ku Klux Klan, *The Invisible Empire,* won the Florida Historical Society's Rembert Patrick Award as "Best Book in Florida History" for 2002. In 2006, the American Library Association honored his *Encyclopedia of Cryptozoology* as one of the year's twelve Outstanding Reference Works. Writing as "Lyle Brandt," Newton won the Western Fictioneers' first Peacemaker Award for Best Western Novel of 2010, for *Manhunt.* Another "Brandt" novel, *Avenging Angels,* was also a Peacemaker Best Novel finalist in 2011, as well as being a Best Paperback Original finalist for the Western Writers of America's Spur Award in 2011. His novel *West of the Big River: The Avenging Angel,* was nominated as a Peacemaker Best Novel in 2014. Newton lives with his wife Heather in Indiana. Readers may contact him by email through his website at *www.michaelnewton.homestead.com*

Amazon Author Page:
http://amzn.to/2duGmJh

Sources

Bill, Vernon. "A trail of butchered girls." *Inside Detective* (September 1973): 20–23, 42–45.

Brannon, W. T. "Did one sex freak kill 24 girls?" *True Detective* (October 1973): 16–21, 63–66.

Cartel, Michael. *Disguise of Sanity: Serial Mass Murderers.* Pepperbox Books, 1985.

—. "I Made a Monster So Mad He Sued Me." (March 9, 2015), http://www.runawaynightmare.com/?p=2095.

"Crime: Bluebeard on the Beach." *Time* (May 28, 1973): 31.

Davidson, Tom. "Man Convicted In Sex Slayings Seeks New Trial." *Sun-Sentinel* (September 19, 1990).

Dorschner, John. "The Devil's Triangle." *Tropic* (January 30, 1994): 7–13, 18–21.

Eaton, R. C. Psychiatric evaluation: Gerard John Schaefer, Jr. (April 10, 1973).

Ellison, Jayne. "6 Dead; 28 May Be: A Trail of Butchered Girls." *Palm Beach Post-Times* (May 13, 1973).

Gerard Schaefer v. Michael Newton and Avon Books 57 F.3d 1073.

Gerard Schaefer v. Michael Newton and Loompanics Unlimited. No. 95-2923, CV-MMP.

Greene, Jessica. "Lake investigators crack a 40-year-old cold case." *Ocala Star-Banner* (July 18, 2007).

Grossman, C., & Bowers, J. "Murder suspect: It will blow over." *Miami Herald,* (May 20, 1973).

Haber, Mordechai. Re: Gerard J. Shaefer [*sic*], Jr. (April 18, 1973).

Harris, Arthur Jay. *Jeffrey Dahmer's Dirty Secret: The Unsolved Murder of Adam Walsh.* The Author, 2009.

—. *Jeffrey Dahmer's Dirty Secret: The "Murder" of Adam Walsh: Finding the Victim.* CreateSpace, 2013.

Killinger, Raymond Jr. Psychological Evaluation of Gerard J. Schaefer Jr. (May 20, 1968).

Lambiet, Jose. "Crime Writer: Adam Walsh is Alive And Well, And Living in Miami!" *Gossip Extra* (March 5, 2015), http://www.gossipextra.com /2014/03/05/adam-walsh-alive-miami-3442.

Michaud, Steven, and Roy Hazelwood. *The Evil That Men Do: FBI Profiler Roy Hazelwood's Journey into the Minds of Sexual Predators.* St. Martin's Press, 1999.

Miller, Frances M. Schaefer, Gerard DC #039506 (March 20. 1985).

Morgan, Willis. *Frustrated Witness: The Story of the Adam Walsh Case and Police Misconduct.* BookBaby, 2015.

Newton, Michael. "Deathwork: Unmasking G. J. Schaefer, the 'Butcher of Blind Creek'," in *Understanding Necrophilia.* Cognella Academic Publishing, 2017, pp. 385-95.

—. "Gerard Schaefer: Hangman." *Serial Killer Quarterly* 2 (Spring 2015): 22-31.

—. *Hunting Humans: An Encyclopedia of Modern Serial Killers.* Loompanics, 1990.

—. *Serial Slaughter: What's Behind America's Murder Epidemic?* Loompanics, 1992.

Norris, Joel. *Serial Killers: The Growing Menace.* Anchor, Doubleday, 1988.

Ogburn, Benjamin R. Consultation Re: Gerard John Schaefer, Jr. (June 20, 1973).

Plarski, Pat. "Killer's Book: Fiction or 'How-To'?" *Palm Beach Post* (August 14, 1989).

Ressler, Robert, and Tom Schachtman. *Whoever Fights Monsters: My Twenty Years Hunting Serial Killers for the FBI.* St. Martin's Press, 1992.

Schaefer, G. J., and Sondra London. *Killer Fiction.* Feral House, 1997.

Schwartz, Anne. *The Man Who Could Not Kill Enough.* Citadel, 1992.

"Skull Identified as Waitress." *Lakeland Ledger* (May 12, 1978).

Stanley, Kameel. "41 years later, killings solved." *Tampa Bay Times* (July 19, 2007).

"Two Murders Linked to 26 Lost, Slain." *Miami News* (May 14, 1973).

Walsh, John. *Tears of Rage.* Atria, 1997.

Wilder, Anne. "Convicted Killer Linked to Dead Iowa Woman." *Miami Herald* (January 19, 1977).

"Writer to Marry Rolling." *New York Times* (February 26, 1993).

Made in the USA
Monee, IL
09 August 2020

37935995R00105